"Tasha Taylor Christian School, High School and Seminary in Pakistan"

پاکستان میں تاشا ٹیلر کرسچن سکول، ہائی سکول اور "
"مدرسہ

"BIBLE STUDIES: DANIEL, DAVID, THE THREE HEBREW BOYS, SAMPSON, JESUS" Fourth Grade Edition (for 9, 10, and 11 year olds)

بائبل اسٹڈیز: ڈینیئل، ڈیوڈ، تین عبرانی لڑکے، سیمپسن، "
"جیسس

Reaping Time Outreach Worship Center and Missions Ministries

Professor: Dr. Tasha Taylor

پروفیسر: ڈاکٹر تاشا ٹیلر

"Table of Contents"

Lesson I. Read the following Passage of Daniel 1 to the students and give them a drawing assignment to illustrate Daniels situation during Daniel Chapter 1. Daniel 1:1-10 says:

سبق .I کے 1 باب ڈینیل انہیں اور پڑھیں حوالہ ذیل مندرجہ کا 1 ڈینیل کو طلباء
ڈینیل۔ دیں اسائنمنٹ ڈرائنگ لیے کے کرنے واضح کو صورتحال کی ڈینیل دوران
ہے کہتا 1:1:-10

Pick two words that are difficult for you to read in the passage define them and write a sentence on them.

1._____

_____

_____

_____

_____

_____

_____2,_____

_____

_____

_____

_____

_____

In the third year of the reign of Jehoiakim king of Judah, Nebuchadnezzar king of Babylon came to Jerusalem and besieged it. ² And the Lord delivered Jehoiakim king of Judah into his hand, along with some of the articles from the temple of God. These he carried off to the temple of his god in Babylonia and put in the treasure house of his god. ³ Then the king ordered Ashpenaz, chief of his court officials, to bring into the king's service some of the Israelites from the royal family and the nobility—

Find two words that are difficult for you to read in this passage and define them.

1._____
_____
_____
_____
_____

2._____
_____
_____
_____
_____

Define these terms in a dictionary:

1. Besieged-

_____

_____

_____

2. Delivered-

_____

_____

_____

3.Temple-

_____

_____

_____

4. articles-

_____

_____

_____

5. house-

_____

_____

_____

6. Treasure-

_____

_____

_____

7. Ordered-

_____

_____

_____

8. Chief-

_____

_____

_____

9. Officials-

_____

_____

_____

10. Nobility-

_____

_____

_____

Please write a sentence for each vocabulary words 1-10 from the last two pages:

1._____

_____

2._____

_____**3.**_____

_____

_____

4_____

_____

5._____

_____

6._____

_____

7._____

_____

8._____

_____

9._____

_____**10.**_____

_____

_____

4 young men without any physical defect, handsome, showing aptitude for every kind of learning, well informed, quick to understand, and qualified to serve in the king's palace. He was to teach them the language and literature of the Babylonians.

یہوداہ کے بادشاہ یہویقیم کی حکومت کے تیسرے سال میں، بابل کا بادشاہ نبوکدنضر یروشلم آیا اور اس کا محاصرہ کر لیا۔ 2 اور خداوند نے یہوداہ کے بادشاہ یہو یقیم کو خدا کی ہیکل کے کچھ سامان سمیت أس کے ہاتھ میں کر دیا۔ ان کو وہ بابل میں اپنے دیوتا کے مندر میں لے گیا اور اپنے دیوتا کے خزانے میں ڈال دیا۔ 3 تب بادشاہ نے اپنے درباری افسروں کے سردار اشپناز کو حکم دیا کہ وہ شاہی خاندان اور شرفاء میں سے کچھ بنی اسرائیل کو بادشاہ کی خدمت میں لے آنے، 4 جوان جو جسمانی عیب کے بغیر، خوبصورت، ہر طرح کی تعلیم کے قابل، خوب صورت تھے۔ باخبر، سمجھنے میں جلدی، اور بادشاہ کے محل میں خدمت کرنے کا اہل۔ وہ انہیں بابلیوں کی زبان اور ادب سکھانا تھا۔

Define the following words:

1. **Physical-**

_____

_____

_____

2. **Handsome-**

_____

_____

_____

3. **Aptitude -**

_____

_____

_____

4. Informed-

_____

_____

_____

5. Language-

_____

_____

_____

Please write a sentence of your own with each of the 5 volcabulary words in them above.

1._____

_____

2._____

_____

3._____

_____

4._____

_____

5._____

_____

5 The king assigned them a daily amount of food and wine from the king's table. They were to be trained for three years, and after that they were to enter the king's service. 6 Among those who were chosen were some from Judah: Daniel, Hananiah, Mishael and Azariah. 7 The chief official gave them new names: to Daniel, the name Belteshazzar; to Hananiah, Shadrach; to Mishael, Meshach; and to Azariah, Abednego.

8 But Daniel resolved not to defile himself with the royal food and wine, and he asked the chief official for permission not to defile himself this way. **9** Now God had caused the official to show favor and compassion to Daniel,

بادشاہ نے اُن کو بادشاہ کے دسترخوان سے روزانہ خوراک اور مئے مقرر کی۔ 5 انہیں تین سال تک تربیت دی جانی تھی اور اس کے بعد انہیں بادشاہ کی خدمت میں حاضر ہونا تھا۔ 6 جن لوگوں کو چنا گیا ان میں کچھ یہوداہ سے تھے: دانیال، حننیاہ، میشاایل اور عزریاہ۔ 7 سردار نے اُن کو نئے نام دیے: دانیال کا نام بیلطشضر۔ حننیاہ، سدرک کو؛ مشائیل، میسک کو؛ اور عزریاہ، عبدنجو کو۔ 8 لیکن دانیال نے شاہی کھانے اور شراب سے اپنے آپ کو ناپاک نہ کرنے کا عزم کیا اور اس نے اعلیٰ افسر سے اجازت مانگی کہ وہ اپنے آپ کو اس طرح ناپاک نہ کرے۔ 9 اب خُدا نے اُس اہلکار کو دانی ایل پر مہربانی اور رحم دلایا تھا۔

10 but the official told Daniel, "I am afraid of my lord the king, who has assigned your food and drink. Why should he see you looking worse than the other young men your age? The king would then have my head because of you."

Translation in Urdo, Daniel 1:1-10

اردو میں ترجمہ، ڈینیئل 1:1-10

لیکن افسر نے دانیال سے کہا، "میں اپنے آقا بادشاہ سے ڈرتا ہوں، جس نے 10 تمہارے کھانے پینے کا انتظام کیا ہے۔ وہ آپ کو اپنی عمر کے دوسرے نوجوانوں سے بدتر کیوں دیکھے؟ بادشاہ تو آپ کی وجہ سے میرا سر پکڑ لے

Picture (Draw a picture of what Daniel might have looked like to you)

تصوير:

1. Please Narrate the importance of being ready for change to the students. In this situation, how was Daniel prepared?   How did Daniel deal with change? Why is it important to deal with change in a Godly fashion?

راہ کرم طلباء کو تبدیلی کے لیے تیار رہنے کی اہمیت بیان کریں۔ اس صورت 10 حال میں، دانیال کیسے تیار تھا؟ دانیال نے تبدیلی سے کیسے نمٹا؟ _____

_____

_____

_____

2. Is Daniel trusting God for his protection? Where does the Bible give inference of Daniels devotion to God in Daniel 1:1-10.

کیا ڈینیل اپنی حفاظت کے لیے خُدا پر بھروسہ کر رہا ہے؟ بائبل ڈینیئل 1: 1-10 میں خدا کے لئے ڈینیئل کی عقیدت کا اندازہ کہاں دیتی ہے۔

_____
_____
_____
_____
_____
_____
_____
_____
_____
_____
_____

2b. How can you give more devotion to God?

_____
_____
_____
____

3. Is Daniel covetous for the wealth of Babylon? Why does he not covet the wealth of Babylon?

کیا دانیال بابل کی دولت کا لالچی ہے؟ وہ بابل کی دولت کا لالچ کیوں نہیں رکھتا؟

_____
_____
_____
_____
_____
_____
_____
_____
_____
_____
_____

3b. Why is it bad to covet?

_____
_____
_____
_____
_____

Are there a few words you do not understand? Look them up
and write a sentence for each word.

1._____
_____

2._____
_____

4. Why is Daniel a trend setter? Discuss with students the
importance of Fasting?

ڈینیل ٹرینڈ سیٹر کیوں ہے؟ روزے کی اہمیت بیان کریں؟

_____
_____
_____
_____
_____
_____
_____
_____
_____
_____
_____

4b. How can you be a trendsetter like Daniel?

_____
_____
_____

Essay:

What dangers does Daniel face growing up as an Orphan in a Strange land that is under captivity of a heathen king?

_____

_____

_____

_____

_____

_____

_____

Lesson II- تفويضII

Lesson II. Please read Daniel chapter 1:11-20 to the students in kindergarten – 1st grade. Have 2nd Graders and up read passages to you. Daniel 1:11-20 says,

براہ کرم کنڈرگارٹن – پہلی جماعت کے طلباء کو ڈینیئل باب 20-1:11 II تفویض گریڈر اور اس سے اوپر کے پاس آپ کو اقتباسات پڑھیں۔ ڈینیل nd -1:11 پڑھیں۔ 2 20، کہتا ہے

_____
_____
_____
_____
_____
_____
_____
_____
_____
_____

"11 Daniel then said to the guard whom the chief official had appointed over Daniel, Hananiah, Mishael and Azariah, 12 "Please test your servants for ten days: Give us nothing but vegetables to eat and water to drink. 13 Then compare our appearance with that of the young men who eat the royal food and treat your servants in accordance with what you see." 14 So he agreed to this and tested them for ten days. 15 At the end of the ten days they looked healthier and better nourished than any of the young men who ate the royal food.

تب دانیال نے اس پہرے سے کہا جسے سردار نے دانیال، حننیاہ، مشائیل اور عزریاہ پر مقرر کیا تھا، 12 "براہ کرم 11 اپنے خادموں کو دس دن تک آزمائیں: ہمیں کھانے کو سبزیاں اور پانی کے سوا کچھ نہ دیں۔ 13 پھر ہماری شکل کا موازنہ ان جوانوں سے کر جو شاہی کھانا کھاتے ہیں اور اپنے خادموں کے ساتھ وہی سلوک کرتے ہیں جو آپ دیکھتے ہیں۔ 14 چنانچہ وہ اس پر راضی ہو گیا اور دس دن تک ان کا امتحان لیا۔ 15 دس دن کے اختتام پر وہ ان جوانوں سے جو شاہی کھانا کھاتے تھے صحت مند اور بہتر نظر آنے۔

_____

_____

_____

_____

_____

_____

_____

_____

_____

_____

_____

16 So the guard took away their choice food and the wine they were to drink and gave them vegetables instead. 17 To these four young men God gave knowledge and understanding of all kinds of literature and learning. And Daniel could understand visions and dreams of all kinds. 18 At the end of the time set by the king to bring them into his service, the chief official presented them to Nebuchadnezzar.

19 The king talked with them, and he found non equal to Daniel, Hananiah, Mishael and Azariah; so they entered the king's service. **20** In every matter of wisdom and understanding about which the king questioned them, he found them ten times better than all the magicians and enchanters in his whole kingdom.

پس پہرے دار نے اُن کی پسند کا کھانا اور مَے جو اُن کو پینی تھی لے گئے 16 اور اُنہیں سبزیاں دیں۔ 17 اِن چاروں جوانوں کو خُدا نے ہر قسم کے ادب اور تعلیم کا علم اور سمجھ عطا کی۔ اور دانیال ہر قسم کے رویا اور خوابوں کو سمجھ سکتا تھا۔ 18 بادشاہ کی طرف سے اُنہیں اپنی خدمت میں لانے کے لیے مقرر کردہ وقت کے اختتام پر، سردار نے اُنہیں نبوکدنضر کے سامنے پیش کیا۔ 19 بادشاہ نے اُن سے بات کی اور اُس نے دانیال، حننیاہ، مشائیل اور عزریاہ کے برابر نہ پایا۔ چنانچہ وہ بادشاہ کی خدمت میں حاضر ہوئے۔ 20 حکمت اور فہم کے ہر معاملے میں جس کے بارے میں بادشاہ نے اُن سے سوال کیا، اُس نے اُن کو اپنی پوری سلطنت کے تمام جادوگروں اور جادوگروں سے دس گنا بہتر پایا۔

(Please Draw) Picture of Daniel's choice of Fruits and Vegetables.

ڈینیل کے پھلوں اور سبزیوں کے انتخاب کی تصویر۔

Place Picture here of Fine foods offered to Daniel, and draw the the officials over Daniel responding to his petition.

ڈینیئل کو پیش کیے گئے گوشت اور کھانوں کی تصویر

Why do you think Daniel refused the food offered to him from King Nebuchadnezzar?

آپ کے خیال میں دانیال نے بادشاہ نبوکدنضر کی طرف سے پیش کردہ کھانے سے انکار کیوں کیا؟

_____
_____
_____
_____
_____
_____
_____
_____
_____
_____
_____
_____

Is it ok to compromise as a Christian? Why or Why not?

If you were in Daniels position, would you have eaten the foods sacrificed to idols?

_____
_____
___

How many days did Daniels Fast last?

دانیال کا روزہ کتنے دن تھا؟

_____
_____
_____

How was Daniel wise and courageous? Please Explain.

دانیال کیسے عقلمند اور دلیر تھا؟ وضاحت کریں.

_____
_____
_____
_____
_____
_____
_____
_____

III.تفويض -.Lesson III

Lesson III. Read Daniel 1:21- Daniel 2:1-9

سبق IIIھ پڑ کو 2:1-9 ڈینیل -1:21 ڈینیل ۔

21. And Daniel remained there until the first year of King Cyrus. In the second year of his reign, Nebuchadnezzar had dreams; his mind was troubled and he could not sleep. 2 So the king summoned the magicians, enchanters, sorcerers and astrologers to tell him what he had dreamed. When they came in and stood before the king, 3 he said to them, "I have had a dream that troubles me and I want to know what it means."

Define these terms:

1. Troubled-

_____

_____

_____

2. Reign-

_____

_____

_____

3.Dream-

_____

_____

_____

Please write a sentence for each of the vocabulary words.

1_____

_____

2._____

_____

3._____

_____

4 Then the astrologers answered the king, "May the king live forever! Tell your servants the dream, and we will interpret it."

اور دانی ایل سائرس بادشاہ کے پہلے سال تک وہیں رہا۔ اپنی حکومت کے 21.
دوسرے سال میں، نبوکدنضر نے خواب دیکھے۔ اس کا دماغ پریشان تھا اور وہ سو
نہیں سکتا تھا۔ 2 چنانچہ بادشاہ نے جادوگروں، جادوگروں، جادوگروں اور نجومیوں
کو بُلا کر بتایا کہ اس نے کیا خواب دیکھا ہے۔ جب وہ اندر آئے اور بادشاہ کے
سامنے کھڑے ہوئے تو اس نے ان سے کہا، "میں نے ایک خواب دیکھا ہے جو
مجھے پریشان کر رہا ہے اور میں جاننا چاہتا ہوں کہ اس کا کیا مطلب ہے۔" 4 تب
نجومیوں نے بادشاہ کو جواب دیا، "بادشاہ ہمیشہ زندہ رہے! اپنے خادموں کو خواب
سناؤ، ہم اس کی تعبیر بیان کریں گے۔"

5 The king replied to the astrologers, "This is what I have firmly decided: If you do not tell me what my dream was and interpret it, I will have you cut into pieces and your houses turned into piles of rubble.

بادشاہ نے نجومیوں کو جواب دیا، "میں نے پختہ فیصلہ کیا ہے کہ اگر تم مجھے 5
یہ نہیں بتاؤ گے کہ میرا خواب کیا تھا اور اس کی تعبیر نہیں بتاؤ گے تو میں تمہیں
ٹکڑے ٹکڑے کر دوں گا اور تمہارے گھر ملبے کے ڈھیر میں

Definition:

1. decided-

_____

_____

_____

____

2.piles-

_____

_____

_____

____

Please write a sentence for each of the vocabulary words.

1._____

_____

2._____

_____

6 But if you tell me the dream and explain it, you will receive from me gifts and rewards and great honor. So tell me the dream and interpret it for me."

لیکن اگر آپ مجھے خواب سنائیں اور اس کی وضاحت کریں تو آپ کو میری طرف سے تحفے اور انعامات اور بڑی عزت ملے گی۔ تو مجھے خواب بتاؤ اور میرے لیے اس کی تعبیر بتاؤ۔

7 Once more they replied, "Let the king tell his servants the dream, and we will interpret it." **8** Then the king answered, "I am certain that you are trying to gain time, because you realize that this is what I have firmly decided: **9** If you do not tell me the dream, there is only one penalty for you. You have conspired to tell me misleading and wicked things, hoping the situation will change. So then, tell me the dream, and I will know that you can interpret it for me."

ایک بار پھر اُنہوں نے جواب دیا، "بادشاہ اپنے خادموں کو خواب سنائے، ہم اُس کی تعبیر بیان کریں گے۔" 8 تب بادشاہ نے جواب دیا، "مجھے یقین ہے کہ تم وقت حاصل کرنے کی کوشش کر رہے ہو، کیونکہ تم جانتے ہو کہ یہ وہی ہے جس کا میں نے پختہ فیصلہ کیا ہے: 9 اگر تم مجھے خواب نہیں بتاؤ گے تو تمہارے لیے صرف ایک ہی سزا ہے۔ تم نے مجھے گمراہ کن اور بری باتیں بتانے کی سازش کی ہے، امید ہے کہ حالات بدل جائیں گے۔ تو پھر مجھے خواب بتاؤ تو مجھے معلوم ہو جائے گا کہ تم میرے لیے اس کی تعبیر کر سکتے ہو۔"

Have students read Daniel 2:10-49 and draw a picture of Daniels revelation of king Nebuchadnezzars dream here. What made Daniels God stand out as being Holy to the king? Picture

تصوير

1. Why does the king choose to have his musicians, astrologers and wise men first tell him the dream and then interpret the dream?

_____

_____

_____

_____

_____

_____

_____

_____

_____

2.Have you ever been deceived? How did you feel about it?

_____

_____

2. Why does Nebuchadnezzar choose to punish his wise men if they cannot tell him the dream that he had (use scripture reference)?

_____

_____

_____

_____

_____

_____

_____

_____

_____

_____

Picture- Read Daniel 3:1-10 and illustrate what this Scripture means to you her

Lesson –IV- تفو

Lesson IV. Daniel Chapter 3:10 – Daniel 3:24

چہارم ڈینیئل باب 3:10 – دانیال 3:24تفویض

10 Your Majesty has issued a decree that everyone who hears the sound of the horn, flute, zither, lyre, harp, pipe and all kinds of music must fall down and worship the image of gold, **11** and that whoever does not fall down, and worship will be thrown into a blazing furnace. **12** But there are some Jews whom you have set over the affairs of the province of Babylon—Shadrach, Meshach and Abednego—who pay no attention to you, Your Majesty. They neither serve your gods nor worship the image of gold you have set up."

مہاراج نے حکم جاری کیا ہے کہ جو کوئی ہارن، بانسری، زیتر، بربط، بربط، 10 پائپ اور ہر قسم کی موسیقی سنتا ہے وہ گر کر سونے کی مورت کو سجدہ کرے، 11 اور یہ کہ جو کوئی گرے نہ گرے۔ عبادت کو بھڑکتی بھٹی میں ڈال دیا جائے گا۔ 12 لیکن کچھ یہودی ہیں جنہیں آپ نے بابل کے صوبے کے معاملات پر مقرر کیا ہے یعنی شدرک، میسک اور عبدنجو، جو آپ کی طرف کوئی توجہ نہیں دیتے۔ وہ نہ تو تمہارے معبودوں کی عبادت کرتے ہیں اور نہ ہی اس سونے کی تصویر کی پوجا کرتے ہیں جسے تم نے بنایا ہے۔ **"11**

Do you Think Daniels Ministry was halted once put In captivity or do you think his Ministry had begun?

_____

_____

_____

_____

_____

_____

_____

_____

_____

_____

_____

_____

_____

13 Furious with rage, Nebuchadnezzar summoned Shadrach, Meshach and Abednego. So these men were brought before the king, 14 and Nebuchadnezzar said to them, "Is it true, Shadrach, Meshach and Abednego, that you do not serve my gods or worship the image of gold I have set up? 15 Now when you hear the sound of the horn, flute, zither, lyre, harp, pipe and all kinds of music, if you are ready to fall down and worship the image I made, very good. But if you do not worship it, you will be thrown immediately into a blazing furnace. Then what god will be able to rescue you from my hand?"

Define these terms:

1.Furious-

_____
_____
_____
____

2.Rage-

_____
_____
_____
____

3. Summoned-

_____

_____

_____

____

4. Worship-

_____

_____

_____

____

غصے میں آکر نبوکدنضر نے شدرک، میسک اور عبدنجو کو بلایا۔ سو اِن 13
آدمیوں کو بادشاہ کے سامنے لایا گیا، 14 اور نبوکدنضر نے اُن سے کہا، "اے
سدرک، میسک اور عبدنجو، کیا یہ سچ ہے کہ تم میرے معبودوں کی عبادت نہیں
کرتے اور اُس سونے کی مورت کی پرستش نہیں کرتے جو میں نے قائم کی ہے؟ب
جب تم بارن، بانسری، زتر، تار، بربط، نلکی اور ہر طرح کی موسیقی سنتے ہو،
اگر تم گر کر میری بنائی ہوئی مورت کو سجدہ کرنے کے لیے تیار ہو، تو بہت اچھا
ہے۔ لیکن اگر تم اس کی پرستش نہیں کرو گے تو تمہیں فوراً بھڑکتی ہوئی بھٹی میں
پھینک دیا جائے گا۔ پھر کون سا خدا تجھے میرے ہاتھ سے چھڑا سکے گا؟

Meshach and Abednego replied to him, "King Nebuchadnezzar, we do not need to defend ourselves before you in this matter. ¹⁷ If we are thrown into the blazing furnace, the God we serve is able to deliver us from it, and he will deliver us from Your Majesty's hand. ¹⁸ But even if he does not, we want you to know, Your Majesty, that we will not serve your gods or worship the image of gold you have set up."

سدرک، میسک اور عبدنجو نے اسے جواب دیا، "بادشاہ نبوکدنضر، ہمیں اس 16 معاملے میں آپ کے سامنے اپنا دفاع کرنے کی ضرورت نہیں ہے۔ 17 اگر ہمیں بھڑکتی ہوئی بھٹی میں ڈال دیا جائے تو خدا جس کی ہم خدمت کرتے ہیں وہ ہمیں

اس سے چھڑانے پر قادر ہے اور وہ تیرے جلال کے ہاتھ سے چھڑائے گا۔ 18 لیکن اگر وہ ایسا نہیں کرتا تو بھی ہم چاہتے ہیں کہ آپ جان لیں کہ ہم آپ کے دیوتاؤں کی عبادت نہیں کریں گے اور نہ ہی آپ کے قائم کردہ سونے کی مورت کی پرستش کریں گے۔

19 Then Nebuchadnezzar was furious with Shadrach, Meshach and Abednego, and his attitude toward them changed. He ordered the furnace heated seven times hotter than usual 20 and commanded some of the strongest soldiers in his army to tie up Shadrach, Meshach and Abednego and throw them into the blazing furnace. 21 So these men, wearing their robes, trousers, turbans and other clothes, were bound and thrown into the blazing furnace.

تب نبوکدنضر سدرک، میسک اور عبدنجو سے غصے میں تھا اور ان کے ساتھ 19 اس کا رویہ بدل گیا۔ اس نے بھٹی کو معمول سے سات گنا زیادہ گرم کرنے کا حکم دیا 20 اور اپنی فوج کے کچھ مضبوط سپاہیوں کو حکم دیا کہ وہ شدرک، میسک اور عبدنجو کو باندھ کر بھڑکتی ہوئی بھٹی میں پھینک دیں۔ 21 پس اُن آدمیوں کو،

جو اپنے لباس، پتلون، پگڑیاں اور دوسرے کپڑے پہنے ہوئے تھے، باندھ کر بھڑکتی ہوئی بھٹی میں ڈال دیا گیا۔

Please define these words:

1.Attitude-

_____
_____
___

2.Toward-

_____
_____
___

3.Furnace-

_____

_____

___

4.Heated-

_____

_____

___

5.Commanded-

_____

_____

___

6.Soldiers-

_____

_____

___

7.Blazing-

_____

_____

___

8.Turbans-

_____

_____

___

22 The king's command was so urgent and the furnace so hot that the flames of the fire killed the soldiers who took up Shadrach, Meshach and Abednego, **23** and these three men, firmly tied, fell into the blazing furnace.

24 Then King Nebuchadnezzar leaped to his feet in amazement and asked his advisers, "Weren't there three men that we tied up and threw into the fire?"

They replied, "Certainly, Your Majesty."

بادشاہ کا حکم بہت ضروری تھا اور بھٹی اتنی گرم تھی کہ آگ کے شعلوں نے 22
ان سپاہیوں کو بلاک کر دیا جنہوں نے سدرک، میسک اور عبدنجو کو اٹھایا، 23
اور یہ تینوں آدمی مضبوطی سے بندھے ہوئے بھڑکتی ہوئی بھٹی میں گر گئے۔

24 تب بادشاہ نبوکدنضر حیران ہو کر اپنے پاؤں پر اچھلا اور اپنے مشیروں سے
پوچھا، "کیا تین آدمی نہیں تھے جنہیں ہم نے باندھ کر آگ میں پھینک دیا؟"

اُنھوں نے جواب دیا، "یقیناً مہاراج"۔

Picture

(Please draw a picture of what the king saw

1. Why did Shadrack Meshack and Abednego defy the kings' orders?

_____

_____

_____

_____

_____

_____

_____

_____

_____
_____
_____
_____

2.   Why is the king astonished? Please give Scriptural
     reference.

_____
_____
_____
_____
_____
_____
_____
_____
_____

3. Who actually perishes because of the fire?

_____

_____

_____

_____

_____

_____

_____

_____

_____

_____

_____

Watch the movie of Daniel with the class.

Then illustrate how this movie makes you feel.

کلاس کے ساتھ دانیال کی فلم دیکھیں۔

پھر وضاحت کریں کہ یہ فلم آپ کو کیسا محسوس کرتی ہے۔

V تفويض -Lesson V

Lesson VI. Daniel 3:25- Daniel 4:6

ڈینیل 3:25- ڈینیل 4:6

25 "He answered and said, Lo, I see four men loose, walking in the midst of the fire, and they have no hurt; and the form of the fourth is like the Son of God.[1]

26 Nebuchadnezzar then approached the opening of the blazing furnace and shouted, "Shadrach, Meshach and Abednego, servants of the Most High God, come out! Come here!"

---

[1] "DANIEL 3:25 KJV 'He Answered and Said, Lo, I See Four Men Loose, Walking in the Midst of the Fire, and They Have No Hurt;...'" *OFFICIAL KING JAMES BIBLE ONLINE: AUTHORIZED KING JAMES VERSION (KJV)*, https://www.kingjamesbibleonline.org/Daniel-3-25/. Accessed 2 Mar. 2023.

So Shadrach, Meshach and Abednego came out of the fire, [27] and the satraps, prefects, governors and royal advisers crowded around them. They saw that the fire had not harmed their bodies, nor was a hair of their heads singed; their robes were not scorched, and there was no smell of fire on them.

اُس نے جواب دیا، دیکھو، مَیں چار آدمیوں کو ڈھیلے ہوتے دیکھتا ہوں، جو آگ کے درمیان چل رہے ہیں، اور اُن کو کوئی چوٹ نہیں لگی۔ اور چوتھے کی شکل خدا کے بیٹے کی طرح ہے۔1

تب نبوکدنضر بھڑکتی ہوئی بھٹی کے قریب آیا اور چلّایا، "شدرک، میسک اور 26 عبدنجو، خداتعالیٰ کے بندو، باہر آؤ! اِدھر آؤ"

سو شدرک، میسک اور عبدنجو آگ سے باہر نکلے، 27 اور حاکموں، حاکموں، گورنروں اور شاہی مشیروں نے اِن کے گرد ہجوم کیا۔ اُنہوں نے دیکھا کہ آگ نے اِن کے جسموں کو نقصان نہیں پہنچایا، نہ اُن کے سر کا ایک بال بھی اُجالا تھا۔ اُن کے کپڑے جلے ہوئے نہیں تھے اور اُن سے آگ کی بو نہیں تھی۔

28 Then Nebuchadnezzar said, "Praise be to the God of Shadrach, Meshach and Abednego, who has sent his angel and rescued his servants! They trusted in him and defied the king's command and were willing to give up their lives rather than serve or worship any god except their own God. **29** Therefore I decree that the people of any nation or language who say anything against the God of Shadrach, Meshach and Abednego be cut into pieces and their houses be turned into piles of rubble, for no other god can save in this way."

تب نبوکدنضر نے کہا، ”شدرک، میسک اور عبدنجو کے خدا کی حمد ہو جس 28 نے اپنا فرشتہ بھیج کر اپنے خادموں کو بچایا۔ انہوں نے اس پر بھروسہ کیا اور بادشاہ کے حکم کی خلاف ورزی کی اور اپنے خدا کے علاوہ کسی معبود کی عبادت یا عبادت کرنے کے بجائے اپنی جان دینے کو تیار تھے۔ 29 اِس لیے مَیں حکم دیتا ہوں کہ کسی بھی قوم یا زبان کے لوگ جو سدرک، میسک اور عبدنجو کے خدا کے خلاف کچھ کہتے ہیں اُن کے ٹکڑے ٹکڑے کر دیے جائیں اور اُن کے گھروں کو ملبے کا ڈھیر بنا دیا جائے، کیونکہ کوئی دوسرا خدا اِس طرح سے بچا نہیں سکتا۔

30 "Then the king promoted Shadrach, Meshach, and Abednego, in the province of Babylon."

1 Nebuchadnezzar the king, unto all people, nations, and languages, that dwell in all the earth; Peace be multiplied unto you.

2. I thought it good to shew the signs and wonders that the high God hath wrought toward me.

تب بادشاہ نے بابل کے صوبے میں سدرک، میسک اور عبدنجو کو ترقی دی۔ 30

نبوکدنضر بادشاہ، تمام لوگوں، قوموں اور زبانوں کو، جو تمام زمین پر بستے ہیں۔ سلامتی آپ کو کئی گنا ہو.

مَیں نے اُن نشانوں اور عجائبات کو ظاہر کرنا اچھا سمجھا جو اعلیٰ خُدا نے 2 میری طرف کیے ہیں۔

3 How great are his signs,
   how mighty his wonders!
His kingdom is an eternal kingdom;
   his dominion endures from generation to generation

4 I, Nebuchadnezzar, was at home in my palace, contented and prosperous. 5 I had a dream that made me afraid. As I was lying in bed, the images and visions that passed through my mind terrified me. 6 So I commanded that all the wise men of Babylon be brought before me to interpret the dream for me.

میں، نبوکدنضر، اپنے محل میں گھر پر تھا، مطمئن اور خوشحال تھا۔ 5 میں نے 4 ایک خواب دیکھا جس نے مجھے خوفزدہ کر دیا۔ جب میں بستر پر لیٹا تھا، میرے ذہن سے گزرنے والی تصویروں اور نظاروں نے مجھے خوفزدہ کر دیا۔ 6 چنانچہ میں نے حکم دیا کہ بابل کے تمام دانشمندوں کو میرے سامنے لایا جائے تاکہ وہ میرے خواب کی تعبیر بتائیں۔

Draw Picture of the Firey furnace

فائر فرنس کی تصویر

1. **What crime did Shadrack, Meshack and Abednego commit?**

_____

_____

_____

_____
_____
_____
_____
_____
_____

2.   **What punishment was given for their crime?**

2.   ان کے جرم کی کیا سزا دی گئی؟

_____
_____
_____

_____

_____

_____

_____

_____

_____

_____

Was the king remorseful for his judgement? When did his decree change?

کیا بادشاہ اپنے فیصلے پر پشیمان تھا؟ اس کا فرمان کب بدلا؟

_____

_____

_____

_____

_____

_____

VI تفويض -Lesson VI

7. When the magicians, enchanters, astrologers and diviners came, I told them the dream, but they could not interpret it for me. **8** Finally, Daniel came into my presence, and I told him the dream. (He is called Belteshazzar, after the name of my god, and the spirit of the holy gods is in him.)

جب جادوگر، جادوگر، نجومی اور ظہور کرنے والے آئے تو میں نے انہیں 7
خواب سنایا، لیکن وہ میرے لیے اس کی تعبیر نہ بتا سکے۔ 8 آخرکار دانیال میرے
سامنے آیا اور میں نے اسے خواب سنایا۔ (وہ میرے معبود کے نام پر بیلتشضر
کہلاتا ہے اور مقدس دیوتاؤں کی روح اس میں ہے۔)

9 I said, "Belteshazzar, chief of the magicians, I know that the spirit of the holy gods is in you, and no mystery is too difficult for you. Here is my dream; interpret it for me. 10 These are the visions I saw while lying in bed: I looked, and there before me stood a tree in the middle of the land. Its height was enormous. 11 The tree grew large and strong and its top touched the sky; it was visible to the ends of the earth.

اے بیلطشضر، جادوگروں کے مالک، کیونکہ میں جانتا ہوں کہ مقدس دیوتاؤں 9
کی روح تجھ میں ہے اور کوئی راز تجھے پریشان نہیں کرتا، مجھے میرے خواب
کی رویا جو میں نے دیکھی ہے اور اس کی تعبیر بتا۔

میرے بستر پر میرے سر کی رویا یوں تھیں۔ میں نے دیکھا، اور زمین کے بیچ 10
میں ایک درخت دیکھا، اور اس کی اونچائی بہت تھی۔

درخت بڑھتا اور مضبوط ہوا اور اس کی اونچائی آسمان تک پہنچ گئی اور اس 11
کی نظر تمام زمین کے آخر تک پہنچ گئی۔

12 The leaves thereof were fair, and the fruit thereof much, and in it was meat for all: the beasts of the field had shadow under it, and the fowls of the heaven dwelt in the boughs thereof, and all flesh was fed of it.

13 I saw in the visions of my head upon my bed, and, behold, a watcher and an holy one came down from heaven;

12 : اُس کے پتے اور اُس کا بہت سا پھل تھا اور اُس میں سب کے لیے گوشت تھا
کھیت کے جانور اُس کے نیچے سایہ کرتے تھے اور آسمان کے پرندے اُس کی
شاخوں میں رہتے تھے اور تمام گوشت اُس سے کھایا جاتا تھا۔ .

13 میں نے اپنے بستر پر اپنے سر کی رویا میں دیکھا، اور دیکھو، ایک نگہبان اور
ایک مقدس آسمان سے نیچے آیا ہے۔

14 He called in a loud voice: 'Cut down the tree and trim off its branches; strip off its leaves and scatter its fruit. Let the animals flee from under it and the birds from its branches. ¹⁵ But let the stump and its roots, bound with iron and bronze, remain in the ground, in the grass of the field.

"'Let him be drenched with the dew of heaven, and let him live with the animals among the plants of the earth. ¹⁶ Let his mind be changed from that of a man and let him be given the mind of an animal, till seven times pass by for him.

اُس نے اونچی آواز میں پکارا، ”درخت کو کاٹ دو اور اس کی شاخوں کو کاٹ 14 دو۔ اس کے پتے اتار کر پھل بکھیر دو۔ جانور اس کے نیچے سے اور پرندے اس کی شاخوں سے بھاگ جائیں۔ 15 لیکن گُونڈ اور اُس کی جڑیں جو لوہے اور پیتل سے بندھے ہوئے ہیں زمین میں، کھیت کی گھاس میں رہیں۔

”اسے آسمان کی شبنم سے بھیگنے دو، اور زمین کے پودوں کے درمیان جانوروں کے ساتھ رہنے دو۔ 16 اُس کی عقل آدمی کی سوچ سے بدل جائے اور اُسے جانور کی عقل دی جائے، یہاں تک کہ اُس کے لیے سات بار گزر جائیں۔

Draw a Picture of the Dream Daniel Interpreted

ڈینیل کی تعبیر شدہ خواب کی تصویر بنائیں

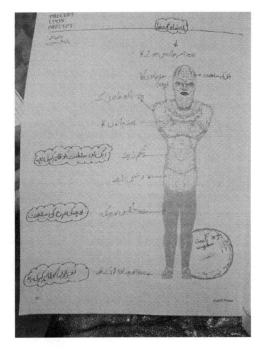

II ESSAY

"How Would You Have Handelled the Decision to bow or be Thrown into the Lions Den" at leasr 5 Chapters for 2nd and third graders, 1t Graders 1 paragraph. Kindergardeners are excused from this assignment.

_____

_____
_____
_____
_____
_____
_____
_____
_____
_____
_____
_____

_____
_____

ESSAY #2:

Why Daniel Celebrated by the King: Please Explain in 5 Paragraphs.

_____

_____

_____

_____

_____

_____

_____

_____

Lesson Daniel V. 4:17-Daniel 4:37

17 "'The decision is announced by messengers, the holy ones declare the verdict, so that the living may know that the Most High is sovereign over all kingdoms on earth and gives them to anyone he wishes and sets over them the lowliest of people.'

18 "This is the dream that I, King Nebuchadnezzar, had. Now, Belteshazzar, tell me what it means, for none of the wise men in my kingdom can interpret it for me. But you can, because the spirit of the holy gods is in you."

فیصلہ کا اعلان رسولوں کے ذریعہ کیا جاتا ہے، مقدس لوگ فیصلہ سناتے " 17 ہیں، تاکہ زندہ لوگ جان لیں کہ حق تعالیٰ زمین کی تمام سلطنتوں پر حاکم ہے اور جسے چاہتا ہے اسے دیتا ہے اور ان پر سب سے ذلیل لوگوں کو مقرر کرتا ہے۔'

18 "یہ وہ خواب ہے جو میں نے، نبوکدنضر بادشاہ نے دیکھا تھا۔ اب، بیلطشضر، مجھے بتاؤ کہ اس کا کیا مطلب ہے، کیونکہ میری بادشاہی کے دانشمندوں میں سے کوئی بھی میرے لیے اس کی تشریح نہیں کر سکتا۔ لیکن تم کر سکتے ہو، کیونکہ "مقدس دیوتاؤں کی روح تم میں ہے۔

Please define these terms:

1.Decision-

_____
_____
_____

____Announce-

_____
_____
_____

_____Declare-

_____
_____
_____

_____Vertict-

_____
_____
_____

_____

[19] Then Daniel (also called Belteshazzar) was greatly perplexed for a time, and his thoughts terrified him. So the king said, "Belteshazzar, do not let the dream or its meaning alarm you."

Belteshazzar answered, "My lord, if only the dream applied to your enemies and its meaning to your adversaries! [20] The tree you saw, which grew large and strong, with its top touching the sky, visible to the whole earth, [21] with beautiful leaves and abundant fruit, providing food for all, giving shelter to the wild animals, and having nesting places in its branches for the birds—

مہاراج، آپ وہ درخت ہیں! تُو عظیم اور مضبوط ہو گیا ہے۔ تیری عظمت بڑھ 22 گئی یہاں تک کہ آسمان تک پہنچ گئی اور تیری سلطنت زمین کے دور دراز تک پھیل گئی۔

23 آپ نے ایک مُقدّس کو دیکھا جو ایک رسول کو آسمان سے اُتر کر کہہ رہا تھا، 'درخت کو کاٹ ڈالو اور اُسے نیست و نابود کر دو، لیکن اُسے لوہے اور پیتل سے بندھا ہوا کھیت کی گھاس میں چھوڑ دو، جب تک اُس کی جڑیں باقی رہیں۔ میدان میں. وہ آسمان کی شبنم سے بھیگ جائے۔ اسے جنگلی جانوروں کے ساتھ رہنے دو، ''یہاں تک کہ اس کے لیے سات وقت گزر جائے۔

Please Define these terms:

1. Perplexed-

_____

_____

_____

_____

2.Terrified-

_____

_____

_____

_____

3.Alarmed-

_____

_____

_____

____

4. Applied-

_____

_____

_____

____

5.Enemies-

_____

_____

____6.Adversaries-

_____

_____

____7. Large-

_____

_____

_____

_____Strong-

_____
_____
_____

_____9. Touching-

_____
_____
_____

_____10. Beautiful-

_____
_____
_____

_____

24 "This is the interpretation, Your Majesty, and this is the decree the Most High has issued against my lord the king: **25** You will be driven away from people and will live with the wild animals; you will eat grass like the ox and be drenched with the dew of heaven. Seven times will pass by for you until you acknowledge that the Most High is sovereign over all kingdoms on earth and gives them to anyone he wishes. **26** The command to leave the stump of the tree with its roots means that your kingdom will be restored to you when you acknowledge that Heaven rules.

اے مہاراج، یہ تعبیر ہے، اور یہ وہ فرمان ہے جو اللہ تعالیٰ نے میرے آقا 24 "
بادشاہ کے خلاف جاری کیا ہے: 25 تم لوگوں سے دور ہو جاؤ گے اور جنگلی

جانوروں کے ساتھ رہو گے۔ تم بیل کی طرح گھاس کھاؤ گے اور آسمان کی اوس سے بھیگ جاؤ گے۔ آپ کے لیے سات زمانے گزر جائیں گے جب تک کہ آپ یہ تسلیم نہ کر لیں کہ سب سے اعلیٰ زمین پر تمام سلطنتوں پر حاکم ہے اور وہ جسے چاہے عطا کرے۔ 26.

Please define the Definitions:

1.Magesty-

_____

_____

_____
____2. Issued-

_____

_____

_____
____3.Drenched-

_____
_____
_____
____

4. Against-
_____
_____
_____

____5.Driven-
_____
_____
_____
____

6. Stump-
_____
_____
_____

____7.Roots-
_____
_____
_____

____8.Record-

_____

_____

_____

_____9. Acknowledge-

_____

_____

_____10. Heaven-

_____

_____

_____

_____

27 Therefore, Your Majesty, be pleased to accept my advice: Renounce your sins by doing what is right, and your wickedness by being kind to the oppressed. It may be that then your prosperity will continue."

28 All this happened to King Nebuchadnezzar. **29** Twelve months later, as the king was walking on the roof of the royal palace of Babylon, **30** he said, "Is not this the great Babylon I have built as the royal residence, by my mighty power and for the glory of my majesty?"

اِس لِئے اَے عَزَّوَجَلَّ، میری نصیحت کو قبول کر کے خوش ہو جا: اپنے گُناہوں کو 27 صحیح کر کے اور اپنی بُرائیوں کو مظالم پر مہربانی کر کے ترک کر۔ ہو سکتا ہے کہ "پھر تمہاری خوشحالی قائم رہے۔

یہ سب کچھ نبوکدنضر بادشاہ کے ساتھ ہوا۔ 29 بارہ مہینے کے بعد، جب بادشاہ بابل 28 کے شاہی محل کی چھت پر چل رہا تھا، 30 اس نے کہا، "کیا یہ وہ عظیم بابل نہیں ہے جسے میں نے اپنی زبردست طاقت اور اپنی عظمت کے جلال کے لیے شاہی رہائش گاہ کے طور

29 At the end of twelve months he walked in the palace of the kingdom of Babylon.

30 The king spake, and said, Is not this great Babylon, that I have built for the house of the kingdom by the might of my power, and for the honour of my majesty?

31 While the word was in the king's mouth, there fell a voice from heaven, saying, O king Nebuchadnezzar, to thee it is spoken; The kingdom is departed from thee.

بارہ مہینے کے آخر میں وہ بابل کی بادشاہی کے محل میں چلا گیا۔ 29

بادشاہ نے کہا، کیا یہ عظیم بابل نہیں ہے جسے میں نے بادشاہی کے گھر کے 30
لیے اپنی طاقت اور اپنی عظمت کی عزت کے لیے بنایا ہے؟

جب بادشاہ کے منہ میں یہ کلام ہو رہا تھا تو آسمان سے ایک آواز آئی کہ اے 31
بادشاہ نبوکدنضر تجھ سے کہا گیا ہے۔ بادشاہی تجھ سے چلی گئی۔

32 You will be driven away from people and will live with the
wild animals; you will eat grass like the ox. Seven times will
pass by for you until you acknowledge that the Most High is
sovereign over all kingdoms on earth and gives them to
anyone he wishes."

33 The same hour was the thing fulfilled upon
Nebuchadnezzar: and he was driven from men, and did eat
grass as oxen, and his body was wet with the dew of heaven,
till his hairs were grown like eagles' feathers, and his nails
like birds' claws.

تم لوگوں سے دور ہو جاؤ گے اور جنگلی جانوروں کے ساتھ رہو گے۔ تم بیل کی 32
طرح گھاس کھاؤ گے۔ سات زمانے آپ کے لیے گزر جائیں گے جب تک کہ آپ یہ تسلیم
نہ کر لیں کہ خدا زمین کی تمام سلطنتوں پر حاکم ہے اور جسے چاہتا ہے عطا کرتا ہے۔"

وہی گھڑی نبوکدنضر پر پوری ہوئی اور وہ آدمیوں سے نکال دیا گیا اور بیلوں کی 33
طرح گھاس کھاتا رہا اور اس کا جسم آسمان کی اوس سے تر ہو گیا یہاں تک کہ اس کے
بال عقاب کے پروں کی طرح اور اس کے ناخن جیسے ہو گئے۔ پرندوں کے پنجے

34 And at the end of the days I Nebuchadnezzar lifted up mine eyes unto heaven, and mine understanding returned unto me, and I blessed the most High, and I praised and honoured him that liveth for ever, whose dominion is an everlasting dominion, and his kingdom is from generation to generation:

35 And all the inhabitants of the earth are reputed as nothing: and he doeth according to his will in the army of heaven, and among the inhabitants of the earth: and none can stay his hand, or say unto him, What doest thou?

اور ایام کے آخر میں نبوکدنضر نے اپنی آنکھیں آسمان کی طرف اٹھائیں اور 34
میری سمجھ مجھ پر لوٹ آئی اور میں نے حق تعالیٰ کو برکت دی اور میں نے اس
کی تعریف اور تعظیم کی جو ابد تک زندہ ہے جس کی بادشاہی ابدی بادشاہی ہے
اور اس کی بادشاہی ایک نسل سے اگلی نسل تک ہے۔

اور زمین کے تمام باشندے کچھ بھی نہیں سمجھے جاتے ہیں: اور وہ آسمان کی 35
فوج میں اور زمین کے باشندوں میں اپنی مرضی کے مطابق کرتا ہے: اور کوئی
اس کا ہاتھ نہیں روک سکتا، یا اس سے کہتا ہے، تم کیا کرتا ہے؟

36 At the same time my reason returned unto me; and for the glory of my kingdom, mine honour and brightness returned unto me; and my counsellors and my lords sought unto me; and I was established in my kingdom, and excellent majesty was added unto me.

37 Now I Nebuchadnezzar praise and extol and honour the King of heaven, all whose works are truth, and his ways judgment: and those that walk in pride he is able to abase.

اسی وقت میری وجہ میرے پاس واپس آئی۔ اور میری بادشاہی کے جلال کے 36
لیے، میری عزت اور چمک میرے پاس لوٹ آئی۔ اور میرے مشیر اور میرے آقا

مجھے ڈھونڈ رہے تھے۔ اور میں اپنی بادشاہی میں قائم ہو گیا، اور میرے لیے بہترین شان و شوکت کا اضافہ کیا گیا۔

37 اب میں نبوکدنضر آسمان کے بادشاہ کی ستائش اور تمجید اور تعظیم کرتا ہوں جس کے تمام کام سچے ہیں اور اس کے طریقے انصاف ہیں اور وہ جو تکبر سے چلتے ہیں ان کو رسوا کر سکتا ہے۔

Lesson Daniel 5:31

5 Belshazzar the king made a great feast to a thousand of his lords, and drank wine before the thousand.

2 Belshazzar, whiles he tasted the wine, commanded to bring the golden and silver vessels which his father Nebuchadnezzar had taken out of the temple which was in Jerusalem; that the king, and his princes, his wives, and his concubines, might drink therein.

3 Then they brought the golden vessels that were taken out of the temple of the house of God which was at Jerusalem; and the king, and his princes, his wives, and his concubines, drank in them.

بیلشضر بادشاہ نے اپنے ایک ہزار آقاوں کی بڑی ضیافت کی اور ہزار کے آگے 5
مئے پی۔

2 بیلشضر نے شراب چکھنے کے دوران سونے اور چاندی کے برتن لانے کا حکم
دیا جو اس کے باپ نبوکدنضر نے یروشلم کی ہیکل سے نکالے تھے۔ کہ بادشاہ، اس
کے شہزادے، اس کی بیویاں اور اس کی لونڈیاں اس میں پیں۔

3 پھر وہ سونے کے برتن لائے جو یروشلم میں خدا کے گھر کی ہیکل سے نکالے
گئے تھے۔ اور بادشاہ، اس کے شہزادے، اس کی بیویاں اور اس کی لونڈیاں ان میں
پیتے تھے۔

In one 5 paragraph Essay Explain Daniesl level of Sacrifice

_____

_____

_____

_____

_____

_____
_____
_____
_____
_____
_____
_____
_____
_____
_____
_____
_____
_____
_____
_____
_____
_____
_____
_____
_____
_____

_____

Prepare for a 5 minute Presintation to the class on the life of Daniel. This exercise is worth 30% of your grade in this class

The Life of David

I Samuel 16

16 And the LORD said unto Samuel, How long wilt thou mourn for Saul, seeing I have rejected him from reigning over Israel? fill thine horn with oil, and go, I will send thee to Jesse the Bethlehemite: for I have provided me a king among his sons.

² And Samuel said, How can I go? if Saul hear it, he will kill me. And the L<small>ORD</small> said, Take an heifer with thee, and say, I am come to sacrifice to the L<small>ORD</small>.

³ And call Jesse to the sacrifice, and I will shew thee what thou shalt do: and thou shalt anoint unto me him whom I name unto thee.

⁴ And Samuel did that which the L<small>ORD</small> spake, and came to Bethlehem. And the elders of the town trembled at his coming, and said, Comest thou peaceably?

⁵ And he said, Peaceably: I am come to sacrifice unto the L<small>ORD</small>: sanctify yourselves, and come with me to the sacrifice. And he sanctified Jesse and his sons, and called them to the sacrifice.

⁶ And it came to pass, when they were come, that he looked on Eliab, and said, Surely the L<small>ORD</small>'s anointed is before him.

⁷ But the L<small>ORD</small> said unto Samuel, Look not on his countenance, or on the height of his stature; because I have refused him: for the L<small>ORD</small> seeth not as man seeth; for man looketh on the outward appearance, but the L<small>ORD</small> looketh on the heart.

⁸ Then Jesse called Abinadab, and made him pass before Samuel. And he said, Neither hath the L<small>ORD</small> chosen this.

⁹ Then Jesse made Shammah to pass by. And he said, Neither hath the L<small>ORD</small> chosen this.

¹⁰ Again, Jesse made seven of his sons to pass before Samuel. And Samuel said unto Jesse, The LORD hath not chosen these.

¹¹ And Samuel said unto Jesse, Are here all thy children? And he said, There remaineth yet the youngest, and, behold, he keepeth the sheep. And Samuel said unto Jesse, Send and fetch him: for we will not sit down till he come hither.

¹² And he sent, and brought him in. Now he was ruddy, and withal of a beautiful countenance, and goodly to look to. And the LORD said, Arise, anoint him: for this is he.

¹³ Then Samuel took the horn of oil, and anointed him in the midst of his brethren: and the Spirit of the LORD came upon David from that day forward. So Samuel rose up, and went to Ramah.

¹⁴ But the Spirit of the LORD departed from Saul, and an evil spirit from the LORD troubled him.

¹⁵ And Saul's servants said unto him, Behold now, an evil spirit from God troubleth thee.

¹⁶ Let our lord now command thy servants, which are before thee, to seek out a man, who is a cunning player on an harp: and it shall come to pass, when the evil spirit from God is upon thee, that he shall play with his hand, and thou shalt be well.

¹⁷ And Saul said unto his servants, Provide me now a man that can play well, and bring him to me.

¹⁸ Then answered one of the servants, and said, Behold, I have seen a son of Jesse the Bethlehemite, that is cunning in playing, and a mighty valiant man, and a man of war, and

prudent in matters, and a comely person, and the LORD is with him.

¹⁹ Wherefore Saul sent messengers unto Jesse, and said, Send me David thy son, which is with the sheep.

²⁰ And Jesse took an ass laden with bread, and a bottle of wine, and a kid, and sent them by David his son unto Saul.

²¹ And David came to Saul, and stood before him: and he loved him greatly; and he became his armourbearer.

²² And Saul sent to Jesse, saying, Let David, I pray thee, stand before me; for he hath found favour in my sight.

²³ And it came to pass, when the evil spirit from God was upon Saul, that David took an harp, and played with his hand: so Saul was refreshed, and was well, and the evil spirit departed from him.

I Samuel 17

16 And the LORD said unto Samuel, How long wilt thou mourn for Saul, seeing I have rejected him from reigning over Israel? fill thine horn with oil, and go, I will send thee to Jesse the Bethlehemite: for I have provided me a king among his sons.

² And Samuel said, How can I go? if Saul hear it, he will kill me. And the LORD said, Take an heifer with thee, and say, I am come to sacrifice to the LORD.

³ And call Jesse to the sacrifice, and I will shew thee what thou shalt do: and thou shalt anoint unto me him whom I name unto thee.

4 And Samuel did that which the LORD spake, and came to Bethlehem. And the elders of the town trembled at his coming, and said, Comest thou peaceably?

5 And he said, Peaceably: I am come to sacrifice unto the LORD: sanctify yourselves, and come with me to the sacrifice. And he sanctified Jesse and his sons, and called them to the sacrifice.

6 And it came to pass, when they were come, that he looked on Eliab, and said, Surely the LORD's anointed is before him.

7 But the LORD said unto Samuel, Look not on his countenance, or on the height of his stature; because I have refused him: for the LORD seeth not as man seeth; for man looketh on the outward appearance, but the LORD looketh on the heart.

8 Then Jesse called Abinadab, and made him pass before Samuel. And he said, Neither hath the LORD chosen this.

9 Then Jesse made Shammah to pass by. And he said, Neither hath the LORD chosen this.

10 Again, Jesse made seven of his sons to pass before Samuel. And Samuel said unto Jesse, The LORD hath not chosen these.

11 And Samuel said unto Jesse, Are here all thy children? And he said, There remaineth yet the youngest, and, behold, he keepeth the sheep. And Samuel said unto Jesse, Send and fetch him: for we will not sit down till he come hither.

12 And he sent, and brought him in. Now he was ruddy, and withal of a beautiful countenance, and goodly to look to. And the LORD said, Arise, anoint him: for this is he.

13 Then Samuel took the horn of oil, and anointed him in the midst of his brethren: and the Spirit of the LORD came upon David from that day forward. So Samuel rose up, and went to Ramah.

14 But the Spirit of the LORD departed from Saul, and an evil spirit from the LORD troubled him.

15 And Saul's servants said unto him, Behold now, an evil spirit from God troubleth thee.

16 Let our lord now command thy servants, which are before thee, to seek out a man, who is a cunning player on an harp: and it shall come to pass, when the evil spirit from God is upon thee, that he shall play with his hand, and thou shalt be well.

17 And Saul said unto his servants, Provide me now a man that can play well, and bring him to me.

18 Then answered one of the servants, and said, Behold, I have seen a son of Jesse the Bethlehemite, that is cunning in playing, and a mighty valiant man, and a man of war, and prudent in matters, and a comely person, and the LORD is with him.

19 Wherefore Saul sent messengers unto Jesse, and said, Send me David thy son, which is with the sheep.

20 And Jesse took an ass laden with bread, and a bottle of wine, and a kid, and sent them by David his son unto Saul.

21 And David came to Saul, and stood before him: and he loved him greatly; and he became his armourbearer.

22 And Saul sent to Jesse, saying, Let David, I pray thee, stand before me; for he hath found favour in my sight.

23 And it came to pass, when the evil spirit from God was upon Saul, that David took an harp, and played with his hand: so Saul was refreshed, and was well, and the evil spirit departed from him.

I Samuel 18

18 And it came to pass, when he had made an end of speaking unto Saul, that the soul of Jonathan was knit with the soul of David, and Jonathan loved him as his own soul.

2 And Saul took him that day, and would let him go no more home to his father's house.

3 Then Jonathan and David made a covenant, because he loved him as his own soul.

4 And Jonathan stripped himself of the robe that was upon him, and gave it to David, and his garments, even to his sword, and to his bow, and to his girdle.

5 And David went out whithersoever Saul sent him, and behaved himself wisely: and Saul set him over the men of war, and he was accepted in the sight of all the people, and also in the sight of Saul's servants.

6 And it came to pass as they came, when David was returned from the slaughter of the Philistine, that the women came out of all cities of Israel, singing and dancing, to meet king Saul, with tabrets, with joy, and with instruments of musick.

7 And the women answered one another as they played, and said, Saul hath slain his thousands, and David his ten thousands.

8 And Saul was very wroth, and the saying displeased him; and he said, They have ascribed unto David ten thousands, and to me they have ascribed but thousands: and what can he have more but the kingdom?

9 And Saul eyed David from that day and forward.

10 And it came to pass on the morrow, that the evil spirit from God came upon Saul, and he prophesied in the midst of the house: and David played with his hand, as at other times: and there was a javelin in Saul's hand.

11 And Saul cast the javelin; for he said, I will smite David even to the wall with it. And David avoided out of his presence twice.

12 And Saul was afraid of David, because the LORD was with him, and was departed from Saul.

13 Therefore Saul removed him from him, and made him his captain over a thousand; and he went out and came in before the people.

14 And David behaved himself wisely in all his ways; and the LORD was with him.

15 Wherefore when Saul saw that he behaved himself very wisely, he was afraid of him.

16 But all Israel and Judah loved David, because he went out and came in before them.

17 And Saul said to David, Behold my elder daughter Merab, her will I give thee to wife: only be thou valiant for me, and fight the LORD's battles. For Saul said, Let not mine hand be upon him, but let the hand of the Philistines be upon him.

18 And David said unto Saul, Who am I? and what is my life, or my father's family in Israel, that I should be son in law to the king?

¹⁹ But it came to pass at the time when Merab Saul's daughter should have been given to David, that she was given unto Adriel the Meholathite to wife.

²⁰ And Michal Saul's daughter loved David: and they told Saul, and the thing pleased him.

²¹ And Saul said, I will give him her, that she may be a snare to him, and that the hand of the Philistines may be against him. Wherefore Saul said to David, Thou shalt this day be my son in law in the one of the twain.

²² And Saul commanded his servants, saying, Commune with David secretly, and say, Behold, the king hath delight in thee, and all his servants love thee: now therefore be the king's son in law.

²³ And Saul's servants spake those words in the ears of David. And David said, Seemeth it to you a light thing to be a king's son in law, seeing that I am a poor man, and lightly esteemed?

²⁴ And the servants of Saul told him, saying, On this manner spake David.

²⁵ And Saul said, Thus shall ye say to David, The king desireth not any dowry, but an hundred foreskins of the Philistines, to be avenged of the king's enemies. But Saul thought to make David fall by the hand of the Philistines.

²⁶ And when his servants told David these words, it pleased David well to be the king's son in law: and the days were not expired.

²⁷ Wherefore David arose and went, he and his men, and slew of the Philistines two hundred men; and David brought their foreskins, and they gave them in full tale to the king,

that he might be the king's son in law. And Saul gave him Michal his daughter to wife.

28 And Saul saw and knew that the LORD was with David, and that Michal Saul's daughter loved him.

29 And Saul was yet the more afraid of David; and Saul became David's enemy continually.

30 Then the princes of the Philistines went forth: and it came to pass, after they went forth, that David behaved himself more wisely than all the servants of Saul; so that his name was much set by.

I Samuel 19

19 And Saul spake to Jonathan his son, and to all his servants, that they should kill David.

2 But Jonathan Saul's son delighted much in David: and Jonathan told David, saying, Saul my father seeketh to kill thee: now therefore, I pray thee, take heed to thyself until the morning, and abide in a secret place, and hide thyself:

3 And I will go out and stand beside my father in the field where thou art, and I will commune with my father of thee; and what I see, that I will tell thee.

4 And Jonathan spake good of David unto Saul his father, and said unto him, Let not the king sin against his servant, against David; because he hath not sinned against thee, and because his works have been to thee-ward very good:

5 For he did put his life in his hand, and slew the Philistine, and the LORD wrought a great salvation for all Israel: thou sawest it, and didst rejoice: wherefore then wilt thou sin against innocent blood, to slay David without a cause?

6 And Saul hearkened unto the voice of Jonathan: and Saul sware, As the LORD liveth, he shall not be slain.

7 And Jonathan called David, and Jonathan shewed him all those things. And Jonathan brought David to Saul, and he was in his presence, as in times past.

8 And there was war again: and David went out, and fought with the Philistines, and slew them with a great slaughter; and they fled from him.

9 And the evil spirit from the LORD was upon Saul, as he sat in his house with his javelin in his hand: and David played with his hand.

10 And Saul sought to smite David even to the wall with the javelin: but he slipped away out of Saul's presence, and he smote the javelin into the wall: and David fled, and escaped that night.

11 Saul also sent messengers unto David's house, to watch him, and to slay him in the morning: and Michal David's wife told him, saying, If thou save not thy life to night, to morrow thou shalt be slain.

12 So Michal let David down through a window: and he went, and fled, and escaped.

13 And Michal took an image, and laid it in the bed, and put a pillow of goats' hair for his bolster, and covered it with a cloth.

14 And when Saul sent messengers to take David, she said, He is sick.

15 And Saul sent the messengers again to see David, saying, Bring him up to me in the bed, that I may slay him.

16 And when the messengers were come in, behold, there was an image in the bed, with a pillow of goats' hair for his bolster.

17 And Saul said unto Michal, Why hast thou deceived me so, and sent away mine enemy, that he is escaped? And Michal answered Saul, He said unto me, Let me go; why should I kill thee?

18 So David fled, and escaped, and came to Samuel to Ramah, and told him all that Saul had done to him. And he and Samuel went and dwelt in Naioth.

19 And it was told Saul, saying, Behold, David is at Naioth in Ramah.

20 And Saul sent messengers to take David: and when they saw the company of the prophets prophesying, and Samuel standing as appointed over them, the Spirit of God was upon the messengers of Saul, and they also prophesied.

21 And when it was told Saul, he sent other messengers, and they prophesied likewise. And Saul sent messengers again the third time, and they prophesied also.

22 Then went he also to Ramah, and came to a great well that is in Sechu: and he asked and said, Where are Samuel and David? And one said, Behold, they be at Naioth in Ramah.

23 And he went thither to Naioth in Ramah: and the Spirit of God was upon him also, and he went on, and prophesied, until he came to Naioth in Ramah.

24 And he stripped off his clothes also, and prophesied before Samuel in like manner, and lay down naked all that day and all that night. Wherefore they say, Is Saul also among the prophets?

The Life of Sampson

Judges Chapter 13

13 And the children of Israel did evil again in the sight of the LORD; and the LORD delivered them into the hand of the Philistines forty years.

2 And there was a certain man of Zorah, of the family of the Danites, whose name was Manoah; and his wife was barren, and bare not.

3 And the angel of the LORD appeared unto the woman, and said unto her, Behold now, thou art barren, and bearest not: but thou shalt conceive, and bear a son.

4 Now therefore beware, I pray thee, and drink not wine nor strong drink, and eat not any unclean thing:

5 For, lo, thou shalt conceive, and bear a son; and no razor shall come on his head: for the child shall be a Nazarite unto God from the womb: and he shall begin to deliver Israel out of the hand of the Philistines.

6 Then the woman came and told her husband, saying, A man of God came unto me, and his countenance was like the countenance of an angel of God, very terrible: but I asked him not whence he was, neither told he me his name:

7 But he said unto me, Behold, thou shalt conceive, and bear a son; and now drink no wine nor strong drink, neither eat any unclean thing: for the child shall be a Nazarite to God from the womb to the day of his death.

8 Then Manoah intreated the LORD, and said, O my Lord, let the man of God which thou didst send come again unto us, and teach us what we shall do unto the child that shall be born.

⁹ And God hearkened to the voice of Manoah; and the angel of God came again unto the woman as she sat in the field: but Manoah her husband was not with her.

¹⁰ And the woman made haste, and ran, and shewed her husband, and said unto him, Behold, the man hath appeared unto me, that came unto me the other day.

¹¹ And Manoah arose, and went after his wife, and came to the man, and said unto him, Art thou the man that spakest unto the woman? And he said, I am.

¹² And Manoah said, Now let thy words come to pass. How shall we order the child, and how shall we do unto him?

¹³ And the angel of the LORD said unto Manoah, Of all that I said unto the woman let her beware.

¹⁴ She may not eat of any thing that cometh of the vine, neither let her drink wine or strong drink, nor eat any unclean thing: all that I commanded her let her observe.

¹⁵ And Manoah said unto the angel of the LORD, I pray thee, let us detain thee, until we shall have made ready a kid for thee.

¹⁶ And the angel of the LORD said unto Manoah, Though thou detain me, I will not eat of thy bread: and if thou wilt offer a burnt offering, thou must offer it unto the LORD. For Manoah knew not that he was an angel of the LORD.

¹⁷ And Manoah said unto the angel of the LORD, What is thy name, that when thy sayings come to pass we may do thee honour?

¹⁸ And the angel of the LORD said unto him, Why askest thou thus after my name, seeing it is secret?

¹⁹ So Manoah took a kid with a meat offering, and offered it upon a rock unto the LORD: and the angel did wonderously; and Manoah and his wife looked on.

²⁰ For it came to pass, when the flame went up toward heaven from off the altar, that the angel of the LORD ascended in the flame of the altar. And Manoah and his wife looked on it, and fell on their faces to the ground.

²¹ But the angel of the LORD did no more appear to Manoah and to his wife. Then Manoah knew that he was an angel of the LORD.

²² And Manoah said unto his wife, We shall surely die, because we have seen God.

²³ But his wife said unto him, If the LORD were pleased to kill us, he would not have received a burnt offering and a meat offering at our hands, neither would he have shewed us all these things, nor would as at this time have told us such things as these.

²⁴ And the woman bare a son, and called his name Samson: and the child grew, and the LORD blessed him.

²⁵ And the Spirit of the LORD began to move him at times in the camp of Dan between Zorah and Eshtaol.

Judges Chapter 14

13 And the children of Israel did evil again in the sight of the LORD; and the LORD delivered them into the hand of the Philistines forty years.

2 And there was a certain man of Zorah, of the family of the Danites, whose name was Manoah; and his wife was barren, and bare not.

3 And the angel of the LORD appeared unto the woman, and said unto her, Behold now, thou art barren, and bearest not: but thou shalt conceive, and bear a son.

4 Now therefore beware, I pray thee, and drink not wine nor strong drink, and eat not any unclean thing:

5 For, lo, thou shalt conceive, and bear a son; and no razor shall come on his head: for the child shall be a Nazarite unto God from the womb: and he shall begin to deliver Israel out of the hand of the Philistines.

6 Then the woman came and told her husband, saying, A man of God came unto me, and his countenance was like the countenance of an angel of God, very terrible: but I asked him not whence he was, neither told he me his name:

7 But he said unto me, Behold, thou shalt conceive, and bear a son; and now drink no wine nor strong drink, neither eat any unclean thing: for the child shall be a Nazarite to God from the womb to the day of his death.

8 Then Manoah intreated the LORD, and said, O my Lord, let the man of God which thou didst send come again unto us, and teach us what we shall do unto the child that shall be born.

9 And God hearkened to the voice of Manoah; and the angel of God came again unto the woman as she sat in the field: but Manoah her husband was not with her.

¹⁰ And the woman made haste, and ran, and shewed her husband, and said unto him, Behold, the man hath appeared unto me, that came unto me the other day.

¹¹ And Manoah arose, and went after his wife, and came to the man, and said unto him, Art thou the man that spakest unto the woman? And he said, I am.

¹² And Manoah said, Now let thy words come to pass. How shall we order the child, and how shall we do unto him?

¹³ And the angel of the LORD said unto Manoah, Of all that I said unto the woman let her beware.

¹⁴ She may not eat of any thing that cometh of the vine, neither let her drink wine or strong drink, nor eat any unclean thing: all that I commanded her let her observe.

¹⁵ And Manoah said unto the angel of the LORD, I pray thee, let us detain thee, until we shall have made ready a kid for thee.

¹⁶ And the angel of the LORD said unto Manoah, Though thou detain me, I will not eat of thy bread: and if thou wilt offer a burnt offering, thou must offer it unto the LORD. For Manoah knew not that he was an angel of the LORD.

¹⁷ And Manoah said unto the angel of the LORD, What is thy name, that when thy sayings come to pass we may do thee honour?

¹⁸ And the angel of the LORD said unto him, Why askest thou thus after my name, seeing it is secret?

¹⁹ So Manoah took a kid with a meat offering, and offered it upon a rock unto the LORD: and the angel did wonderously; and Manoah and his wife looked on.

20 For it came to pass, when the flame went up toward heaven from off the altar, that the angel of the LORD ascended in the flame of the altar. And Manoah and his wife looked on it, and fell on their faces to the ground.

21 But the angel of the LORD did no more appear to Manoah and to his wife. Then Manoah knew that he was an angel of the LORD.

22 And Manoah said unto his wife, We shall surely die, because we have seen God.

23 But his wife said unto him, If the LORD were pleased to kill us, he would not have received a burnt offering and a meat offering at our hands, neither would he have shewed us all these things, nor would as at this time have told us such things as these.

24 And the woman bare a son, and called his name Samson: and the child grew, and the LORD blessed him.

25 And the Spirit of the LORD began to move him at times in the camp of Dan between Zorah and Eshtaol.

Judges Chapter 15

13 And the children of Israel did evil again in the sight of the LORD; and the LORD delivered them into the hand of the Philistines forty years.

2 And there was a certain man of Zorah, of the family of the Danites, whose name was Manoah; and his wife was barren, and bare not.

3 And the angel of the LORD appeared unto the woman, and said unto her, Behold now, thou art barren, and bearest not: but thou shalt conceive, and bear a son.

4 Now therefore beware, I pray thee, and drink not wine nor strong drink, and eat not any unclean thing:

5 For, lo, thou shalt conceive, and bear a son; and no razor shall come on his head: for the child shall be a Nazarite unto God from the womb: and he shall begin to deliver Israel out of the hand of the Philistines.

6 Then the woman came and told her husband, saying, A man of God came unto me, and his countenance was like the countenance of an angel of God, very terrible: but I asked him not whence he was, neither told he me his name:

7 But he said unto me, Behold, thou shalt conceive, and bear a son; and now drink no wine nor strong drink, neither eat any unclean thing: for the child shall be a Nazarite to God from the womb to the day of his death.

8 Then Manoah intreated the LORD, and said, O my Lord, let the man of God which thou didst send come again unto us, and teach us what we shall do unto the child that shall be born.

9 And God hearkened to the voice of Manoah; and the angel of God came again unto the woman as she sat in the field: but Manoah her husband was not with her.

10 And the woman made haste, and ran, and shewed her husband, and said unto him, Behold, the man hath appeared unto me, that came unto me the other day.

¹¹ And Manoah arose, and went after his wife, and came to the man, and said unto him, Art thou the man that spakest unto the woman? And he said, I am.

¹² And Manoah said, Now let thy words come to pass. How shall we order the child, and how shall we do unto him?

¹³ And the angel of the LORD said unto Manoah, Of all that I said unto the woman let her beware.

¹⁴ She may not eat of any thing that cometh of the vine, neither let her drink wine or strong drink, nor eat any unclean thing: all that I commanded her let her observe.

¹⁵ And Manoah said unto the angel of the LORD, I pray thee, let us detain thee, until we shall have made ready a kid for thee.

¹⁶ And the angel of the LORD said unto Manoah, Though thou detain me, I will not eat of thy bread: and if thou wilt offer a burnt offering, thou must offer it unto the LORD. For Manoah knew not that he was an angel of the LORD.

¹⁷ And Manoah said unto the angel of the LORD, What is thy name, that when thy sayings come to pass we may do thee honour?

¹⁸ And the angel of the LORD said unto him, Why askest thou thus after my name, seeing it is secret?

¹⁹ So Manoah took a kid with a meat offering, and offered it upon a rock unto the LORD: and the angel did wonderously; and Manoah and his wife looked on.

²⁰ For it came to pass, when the flame went up toward heaven from off the altar, that the angel of the LORD ascended in the flame of the altar. And Manoah and his wife looked on it, and fell on their faces to the ground.

21 But the angel of the LORD did no more appear to Manoah and to his wife. Then Manoah knew that he was an angel of the LORD.

22 And Manoah said unto his wife, We shall surely die, because we have seen God.

23 But his wife said unto him, If the LORD were pleased to kill us, he would not have received a burnt offering and a meat offering at our hands, neither would he have shewed us all these things, nor would as at this time have told us such things as these.

24 And the woman bare a son, and called his name Samson: and the child grew, and the LORD blessed him.

25 And the Spirit of the LORD began to move him at times in the camp of Dan between Zorah and Eshtaol.

Judges Chapter 16

15 But it came to pass within a while after, in the time of wheat harvest, that Samson visited his wife with a kid; and he said, I will go in to my wife into the chamber. But her father would not suffer him to go in.

2 And her father said, I verily thought that thou hadst utterly hated her; therefore I gave her to thy companion: is not her younger sister fairer than she? take her, I pray thee, instead of her.

3 And Samson said concerning them, Now shall I be more blameless than the Philistines, though I do them a displeasure.

4 And Samson went and caught three hundred foxes, and took firebrands, and turned tail to tail, and put a firebrand in the midst between two tails.

5 And when he had set the brands on fire, he let them go into the standing corn of the Philistines, and burnt up both the shocks, and also the standing corn, with the vineyards and olives.

6 Then the Philistines said, Who hath done this? And they answered, Samson, the son in law of the Timnite, because he had taken his wife, and given her to his companion. And the Philistines came up, and burnt her and her father with fire.

7 And Samson said unto them, Though ye have done this, yet will I be avenged of you, and after that I will cease.

8 And he smote them hip and thigh with a great slaughter: and he went down and dwelt in the top of the rock Etam.

9 Then the Philistines went up, and pitched in Judah, and spread themselves in Lehi.

10 And the men of Judah said, Why are ye come up against us? And they answered, To bind Samson are we come up, to do to him as he hath done to us.

11 Then three thousand men of Judah went to the top of the rock Etam, and said to Samson, Knowest thou not that the Philistines are rulers over us? what is this that thou hast done unto us? And he said unto them, As they did unto me, so have I done unto them.

12 And they said unto him, We are come down to bind thee, that we may deliver thee into the hand of the Philistines. And Samson said unto them, Swear unto me, that ye will not fall upon me yourselves.

13 And they spake unto him, saying, No; but we will bind thee fast, and deliver thee into their hand: but surely we will not kill thee. And they bound him with two new cords, and brought him up from the rock.

14 And when he came unto Lehi, the Philistines shouted against him: and the Spirit of the LORD came mightily upon him, and the cords that were upon his arms became as flax that was burnt with fire, and his bands loosed from off his hands.

15 And he found a new jawbone of an ass, and put forth his hand, and took it, and slew a thousand men therewith.

16 And Samson said, With the jawbone of an ass, heaps upon heaps, with the jaw of an ass have I slain a thousand men.

17 And it came to pass, when he had made an end of speaking, that he cast away the jawbone out of his hand, and called that place Ramathlehi.

18 And he was sore athirst, and called on the LORD, and said, Thou hast given this great deliverance into the hand of thy servant: and now shall I die for thirst, and fall into the hand of the uncircumcised?

19 But God clave an hollow place that was in the jaw, and there came water thereout; and when he had drunk, his spirit came again, and he revived: wherefore he called the name thereof Enhakkore, which is in Lehi unto this day.

20 And he judged Israel in the days of the Philistines twenty years.

1. How has the life of Sampson influenced the Isreal culture in his day?
2. Did his choices help or hurt his community. Read the life of Sampson and prepare a 3 page Paper including how you feel his life help or hurt his community. Focus on the idea of choices as you read the book of Judges

Dear students, I pray you prosper and be in health as your soul propers (I pharaphrase.)[2] Study, study, study and I know that God will reward your efforts as you continue to study to show yourself approved a workman rightly dividing the Word of Truth that need not be ashamed.[3]

The Life of our Lord and Savior Jesus Christ.

19 And Saul spake to Jonathan his son, and to all his servants, that they should kill David.

2 But Jonathan Saul's son delighted much in David: and Jonathan told David, saying, Saul my father seeketh to kill

---

[2] "**3 John 1:2 KJV: Beloved, I Wish above All Things That Thou Mayest Prosper and Be in Health, Even as Thy Soul Prospereth.**" *Bible Hub: Search, Read, Study the Bible in Many Languages*, https://biblehub.com/kjv/3_john/1-2.htm. Accessed 3 Mar. 2023.

[3] "**2 Timothy 2:15 - Do Your Best to Present Yourself to God - Bible Gateway.**" *Bible Gateway*, https://www.biblegateway.com/passage/?search=2 Timothy 2:15. Accessed 3 Mar. 2023.

thee: now therefore, I pray thee, take heed to thyself until the morning, and abide in a secret place, and hide thyself:

3 And I will go out and stand beside my father in the field where thou art, and I will commune with my father of thee; and what I see, that I will tell thee.

4 And Jonathan spake good of David unto Saul his father, and said unto him, Let not the king sin against his servant, against David; because he hath not sinned against thee, and because his works have been to thee-ward very good:

5 For he did put his life in his hand, and slew the Philistine, and the LORD wrought a great salvation for all Israel: thou sawest it, and didst rejoice: wherefore then wilt thou sin against innocent blood, to slay David without a cause?

6 And Saul hearkened unto the voice of Jonathan: and Saul sware, As the LORD liveth, he shall not be slain.

7 And Jonathan called David, and Jonathan shewed him all those things. And Jonathan brought David to Saul, and he was in his presence, as in times past.

8 And there was war again: and David went out, and fought with the Philistines, and slew them with a great slaughter; and they fled from him.

9 And the evil spirit from the LORD was upon Saul, as he sat in his house with his javelin in his hand: and David played with his hand.

10 And Saul sought to smite David even to the wall with the javelin: but he slipped away out of Saul's presence, and he smote the javelin into the wall: and David fled, and escaped that night.

11 Saul also sent messengers unto David's house, to watch him, and to slay him in the morning: and Michal David's wife told him, saying, If thou save not thy life to night, to morrow thou shalt be slain.

12 So Michal let David down through a window: and he went, and fled, and escaped.

13 And Michal took an image, and laid it in the bed, and put a pillow of goats' hair for his bolster, and covered it with a cloth.

14 And when Saul sent messengers to take David, she said, He is sick.

15 And Saul sent the messengers again to see David, saying, Bring him up to me in the bed, that I may slay him.

16 And when the messengers were come in, behold, there was an image in the bed, with a pillow of goats' hair for his bolster.

17 And Saul said unto Michal, Why hast thou deceived me so, and sent away mine enemy, that he is escaped? And Michal answered Saul, He said unto me, Let me go; why should I kill thee?

18 So David fled, and escaped, and came to Samuel to Ramah, and told him all that Saul had done to him. And he and Samuel went and dwelt in Naioth.

19 And it was told Saul, saying, Behold, David is at Naioth in Ramah.

20 And Saul sent messengers to take David: and when they saw the company of the prophets prophesying, and Samuel standing as appointed over them, the Spirit of God was upon the messengers of Saul, and they also prophesied.

21 And when it was told Saul, he sent other messengers, and they prophesied likewise. And Saul sent messengers again the third time, and they prophesied also.

22 Then went he also to Ramah, and came to a great well that is in Sechu: and he asked and said, Where are Samuel and David? And one said, Behold, they be at Naioth in Ramah.

23 And he went thither to Naioth in Ramah: and the Spirit of God was upon him also, and he went on, and prophesied, until he came to Naioth in Ramah.

24 And he stripped off his clothes also, and prophesied before Samuel in like manner, and lay down naked all that day and all that night. Wherefore they say, Is Saul also among the prophets?

John 2

19 And Saul spake to Jonathan his son, and to all his servants, that they should kill David.

2 But Jonathan Saul's son delighted much in David: and Jonathan told David, saying, Saul my father seeketh to kill thee: now therefore, I pray thee, take heed to thyself until the morning, and abide in a secret place, and hide thyself:

3 And I will go out and stand beside my father in the field where thou art, and I will commune with my father of thee; and what I see, that I will tell thee.

4 And Jonathan spake good of David unto Saul his father, and said unto him, Let not the king sin against his servant, against David; because he hath not sinned against thee, and because his works have been to thee-ward very good:

5 For he did put his life in his hand, and slew the Philistine, and the LORD wrought a great salvation for all Israel: thou sawest it, and didst rejoice: wherefore then wilt thou sin against innocent blood, to slay David without a cause?

6 And Saul hearkened unto the voice of Jonathan: and Saul sware, As the LORD liveth, he shall not be slain.

7 And Jonathan called David, and Jonathan shewed him all those things. And Jonathan brought David to Saul, and he was in his presence, as in times past.

8 And there was war again: and David went out, and fought with the Philistines, and slew them with a great slaughter; and they fled from him.

9 And the evil spirit from the LORD was upon Saul, as he sat in his house with his javelin in his hand: and David played with his hand.

10 And Saul sought to smite David even to the wall with the javelin: but he slipped away out of Saul's presence, and he smote the javelin into the wall: and David fled, and escaped that night.

11 Saul also sent messengers unto David's house, to watch him, and to slay him in the morning: and Michal David's wife told him, saying, If thou save not thy life to night, to morrow thou shalt be slain.

12 So Michal let David down through a window: and he went, and fled, and escaped.

13 And Michal took an image, and laid it in the bed, and put a pillow of goats' hair for his bolster, and covered it with a cloth.

14 And when Saul sent messengers to take David, she said, He is sick.

¹⁵ And Saul sent the messengers again to see David, saying, Bring him up to me in the bed, that I may slay him.

¹⁶ And when the messengers were come in, behold, there was an image in the bed, with a pillow of goats' hair for his bolster.

¹⁷ And Saul said unto Michal, Why hast thou deceived me so, and sent away mine enemy, that he is escaped? And Michal answered Saul, He said unto me, Let me go; why should I kill thee?

¹⁸ So David fled, and escaped, and came to Samuel to Ramah, and told him all that Saul had done to him. And he and Samuel went and dwelt in Naioth.

¹⁹ And it was told Saul, saying, Behold, David is at Naioth in Ramah.

²⁰ And Saul sent messengers to take David: and when they saw the company of the prophets prophesying, and Samuel standing as appointed over them, the Spirit of God was upon the messengers of Saul, and they also prophesied.

²¹ And when it was told Saul, he sent other messengers, and they prophesied likewise. And Saul sent messengers again the third time, and they prophesied also.

²² Then went he also to Ramah, and came to a great well that is in Sechu: and he asked and said, Where are Samuel and David? And one said, Behold, they be at Naioth in Ramah.

²³ And he went thither to Naioth in Ramah: and the Spirit of God was upon him also, and he went on, and prophesied, until he came to Naioth in Ramah.

²⁴ And he stripped off his clothes also, and prophesied before Samuel in like manner, and lay down naked all that day and

all that night. Wherefore they say, Is Saul also among the prophets?

John 3

19 And Saul spake to Jonathan his son, and to all his servants, that they should kill David.

2 But Jonathan Saul's son delighted much in David: and Jonathan told David, saying, Saul my father seeketh to kill thee: now therefore, I pray thee, take heed to thyself until the morning, and abide in a secret place, and hide thyself:

3 And I will go out and stand beside my father in the field where thou art, and I will commune with my father of thee; and what I see, that I will tell thee.

4 And Jonathan spake good of David unto Saul his father, and said unto him, Let not the king sin against his servant, against David; because he hath not sinned against thee, and because his works have been to thee-ward very good:

5 For he did put his life in his hand, and slew the Philistine, and the LORD wrought a great salvation for all Israel: thou sawest it, and didst rejoice: wherefore then wilt thou sin against innocent blood, to slay David without a cause?

6 And Saul hearkened unto the voice of Jonathan: and Saul sware, As the LORD liveth, he shall not be slain.

7 And Jonathan called David, and Jonathan shewed him all those things. And Jonathan brought David to Saul, and he was in his presence, as in times past.

8 And there was war again: and David went out, and fought with the Philistines, and slew them with a great slaughter; and they fled from him.

⁹ And the evil spirit from the LORD was upon Saul, as he sat in his house with his javelin in his hand: and David played with his hand.

¹⁰ And Saul sought to smite David even to the wall with the javelin: but he slipped away out of Saul's presence, and he smote the javelin into the wall: and David fled, and escaped that night.

¹¹ Saul also sent messengers unto David's house, to watch him, and to slay him in the morning: and Michal David's wife told him, saying, If thou save not thy life to night, to morrow thou shalt be slain.

¹² So Michal let David down through a window: and he went, and fled, and escaped.

¹³ And Michal took an image, and laid it in the bed, and put a pillow of goats' hair for his bolster, and covered it with a cloth.

¹⁴ And when Saul sent messengers to take David, she said, He is sick.

¹⁵ And Saul sent the messengers again to see David, saying, Bring him up to me in the bed, that I may slay him.

¹⁶ And when the messengers were come in, behold, there was an image in the bed, with a pillow of goats' hair for his bolster.

¹⁷ And Saul said unto Michal, Why hast thou deceived me so, and sent away mine enemy, that he is escaped? And Michal answered Saul, He said unto me, Let me go; why should I kill thee?

¹⁸ So David fled, and escaped, and came to Samuel to Ramah, and told him all that Saul had done to him. And he and Samuel went and dwelt in Naioth.

¹⁹ And it was told Saul, saying, Behold, David is at Naioth in Ramah.

²⁰ And Saul sent messengers to take David: and when they saw the company of the prophets prophesying, and Samuel standing as appointed over them, the Spirit of God was upon the messengers of Saul, and they also prophesied.

²¹ And when it was told Saul, he sent other messengers, and they prophesied likewise. And Saul sent messengers again the third time, and they prophesied also.

²² Then went he also to Ramah, and came to a great well that is in Sechu: and he asked and said, Where are Samuel and David? And one said, Behold, they be at Naioth in Ramah.

²³ And he went thither to Naioth in Ramah: and the Spirit of God was upon him also, and he went on, and prophesied, until he came to Naioth in Ramah.

²⁴ And he stripped off his clothes also, and prophesied before Samuel in like manner, and lay down naked all that day and all that night. Wherefore they say, Is Saul also among the prophets?

John 4

19 And Saul spake to Jonathan his son, and to all his servants, that they should kill David.

² But Jonathan Saul's son delighted much in David: and Jonathan told David, saying, Saul my father seeketh to kill

thee: now therefore, I pray thee, take heed to thyself until the morning, and abide in a secret place, and hide thyself:

3 And I will go out and stand beside my father in the field where thou art, and I will commune with my father of thee; and what I see, that I will tell thee.

4 And Jonathan spake good of David unto Saul his father, and said unto him, Let not the king sin against his servant, against David; because he hath not sinned against thee, and because his works have been to thee-ward very good:

5 For he did put his life in his hand, and slew the Philistine, and the LORD wrought a great salvation for all Israel: thou sawest it, and didst rejoice: wherefore then wilt thou sin against innocent blood, to slay David without a cause?

6 And Saul hearkened unto the voice of Jonathan: and Saul sware, As the LORD liveth, he shall not be slain.

7 And Jonathan called David, and Jonathan shewed him all those things. And Jonathan brought David to Saul, and he was in his presence, as in times past.

8 And there was war again: and David went out, and fought with the Philistines, and slew them with a great slaughter; and they fled from him.

9 And the evil spirit from the LORD was upon Saul, as he sat in his house with his javelin in his hand: and David played with his hand.

10 And Saul sought to smite David even to the wall with the javelin: but he slipped away out of Saul's presence, and he smote the javelin into the wall: and David fled, and escaped that night.

11 Saul also sent messengers unto David's house, to watch him, and to slay him in the morning: and Michal David's wife told him, saying, If thou save not thy life to night, to morrow thou shalt be slain.

12 So Michal let David down through a window: and he went, and fled, and escaped.

13 And Michal took an image, and laid it in the bed, and put a pillow of goats' hair for his bolster, and covered it with a cloth.

14 And when Saul sent messengers to take David, she said, He is sick.

15 And Saul sent the messengers again to see David, saying, Bring him up to me in the bed, that I may slay him.

16 And when the messengers were come in, behold, there was an image in the bed, with a pillow of goats' hair for his bolster.

17 And Saul said unto Michal, Why hast thou deceived me so, and sent away mine enemy, that he is escaped? And Michal answered Saul, He said unto me, Let me go; why should I kill thee?

18 So David fled, and escaped, and came to Samuel to Ramah, and told him all that Saul had done to him. And he and Samuel went and dwelt in Naioth.

19 And it was told Saul, saying, Behold, David is at Naioth in Ramah.

20 And Saul sent messengers to take David: and when they saw the company of the prophets prophesying, and Samuel standing as appointed over them, the Spirit of God was upon the messengers of Saul, and they also prophesied.

²¹ And when it was told Saul, he sent other messengers, and they prophesied likewise. And Saul sent messengers again the third time, and they prophesied also.

²² Then went he also to Ramah, and came to a great well that is in Sechu: and he asked and said, Where are Samuel and David? And one said, Behold, they be at Naioth in Ramah.

²³ And he went thither to Naioth in Ramah: and the Spirit of God was upon him also, and he went on, and prophesied, until he came to Naioth in Ramah.

²⁴ And he stripped off his clothes also, and prophesied before Samuel in like manner, and lay down naked all that day and all that night. Wherefore they say, Is Saul also among the prophets?

John 5

19 And Saul spake to Jonathan his son, and to all his servants, that they should kill David.

² But Jonathan Saul's son delighted much in David: and Jonathan told David, saying, Saul my father seeketh to kill thee: now therefore, I pray thee, take heed to thyself until the morning, and abide in a secret place, and hide thyself:

³ And I will go out and stand beside my father in the field where thou art, and I will commune with my father of thee; and what I see, that I will tell thee.

⁴ And Jonathan spake good of David unto Saul his father, and said unto him, Let not the king sin against his servant, against David; because he hath not sinned against thee, and because his works have been to thee-ward very good:

5 For he did put his life in his hand, and slew the Philistine, and the LORD wrought a great salvation for all Israel: thou sawest it, and didst rejoice: wherefore then wilt thou sin against innocent blood, to slay David without a cause?

6 And Saul hearkened unto the voice of Jonathan: and Saul sware, As the LORD liveth, he shall not be slain.

7 And Jonathan called David, and Jonathan shewed him all those things. And Jonathan brought David to Saul, and he was in his presence, as in times past.

8 And there was war again: and David went out, and fought with the Philistines, and slew them with a great slaughter; and they fled from him.

9 And the evil spirit from the LORD was upon Saul, as he sat in his house with his javelin in his hand: and David played with his hand.

10 And Saul sought to smite David even to the wall with the javelin: but he slipped away out of Saul's presence, and he smote the javelin into the wall: and David fled, and escaped that night.

11 Saul also sent messengers unto David's house, to watch him, and to slay him in the morning: and Michal David's wife told him, saying, If thou save not thy life to night, to morrow thou shalt be slain.

12 So Michal let David down through a window: and he went, and fled, and escaped.

13 And Michal took an image, and laid it in the bed, and put a pillow of goats' hair for his bolster, and covered it with a cloth.

14 And when Saul sent messengers to take David, she said, He is sick.

15 And Saul sent the messengers again to see David, saying, Bring him up to me in the bed, that I may slay him.

16 And when the messengers were come in, behold, there was an image in the bed, with a pillow of goats' hair for his bolster.

17 And Saul said unto Michal, Why hast thou deceived me so, and sent away mine enemy, that he is escaped? And Michal answered Saul, He said unto me, Let me go; why should I kill thee?

18 So David fled, and escaped, and came to Samuel to Ramah, and told him all that Saul had done to him. And he and Samuel went and dwelt in Naioth.

19 And it was told Saul, saying, Behold, David is at Naioth in Ramah.

20 And Saul sent messengers to take David: and when they saw the company of the prophets prophesying, and Samuel standing as appointed over them, the Spirit of God was upon the messengers of Saul, and they also prophesied.

21 And when it was told Saul, he sent other messengers, and they prophesied likewise. And Saul sent messengers again the third time, and they prophesied also.

22 Then went he also to Ramah, and came to a great well that is in Sechu: and he asked and said, Where are Samuel and David? And one said, Behold, they be at Naioth in Ramah.

23 And he went thither to Naioth in Ramah: and the Spirit of God was upon him also, and he went on, and prophesied, until he came to Naioth in Ramah.

²⁴ And he stripped off his clothes also, and prophesied before Samuel in like manner, and lay down naked all that day and all that night. Wherefore they say, Is Saul also among the prophets?

John 6

19 And Saul spake to Jonathan his son, and to all his servants, that they should kill David.

² But Jonathan Saul's son delighted much in David: and Jonathan told David, saying, Saul my father seeketh to kill thee: now therefore, I pray thee, take heed to thyself until the morning, and abide in a secret place, and hide thyself:

³ And I will go out and stand beside my father in the field where thou art, and I will commune with my father of thee; and what I see, that I will tell thee.

⁴ And Jonathan spake good of David unto Saul his father, and said unto him, Let not the king sin against his servant, against David; because he hath not sinned against thee, and because his works have been to thee-ward very good:

⁵ For he did put his life in his hand, and slew the Philistine, and the LORD wrought a great salvation for all Israel: thou sawest it, and didst rejoice: wherefore then wilt thou sin against innocent blood, to slay David without a cause?

⁶ And Saul hearkened unto the voice of Jonathan: and Saul sware, As the LORD liveth, he shall not be slain.

⁷ And Jonathan called David, and Jonathan shewed him all those things. And Jonathan brought David to Saul, and he was in his presence, as in times past.

8 And there was war again: and David went out, and fought with the Philistines, and slew them with a great slaughter; and they fled from him.

9 And the evil spirit from the LORD was upon Saul, as he sat in his house with his javelin in his hand: and David played with his hand.

10 And Saul sought to smite David even to the wall with the javelin: but he slipped away out of Saul's presence, and he smote the javelin into the wall: and David fled, and escaped that night.

11 Saul also sent messengers unto David's house, to watch him, and to slay him in the morning: and Michal David's wife told him, saying, If thou save not thy life to night, to morrow thou shalt be slain.

12 So Michal let David down through a window: and he went, and fled, and escaped.

13 And Michal took an image, and laid it in the bed, and put a pillow of goats' hair for his bolster, and covered it with a cloth.

14 And when Saul sent messengers to take David, she said, He is sick.

15 And Saul sent the messengers again to see David, saying, Bring him up to me in the bed, that I may slay him.

16 And when the messengers were come in, behold, there was an image in the bed, with a pillow of goats' hair for his bolster.

17 And Saul said unto Michal, Why hast thou deceived me so, and sent away mine enemy, that he is escaped? And Michal answered Saul, He said unto me, Let me go; why should I kill thee?

18 So David fled, and escaped, and came to Samuel to Ramah, and told him all that Saul had done to him. And he and Samuel went and dwelt in Naioth.

19 And it was told Saul, saying, Behold, David is at Naioth in Ramah.

20 And Saul sent messengers to take David: and when they saw the company of the prophets prophesying, and Samuel standing as appointed over them, the Spirit of God was upon the messengers of Saul, and they also prophesied.

21 And when it was told Saul, he sent other messengers, and they prophesied likewise. And Saul sent messengers again the third time, and they prophesied also.

22 Then went he also to Ramah, and came to a great well that is in Sechu: and he asked and said, Where are Samuel and David? And one said, Behold, they be at Naioth in Ramah.

23 And he went thither to Naioth in Ramah: and the Spirit of God was upon him also, and he went on, and prophesied, until he came to Naioth in Ramah.

24 And he stripped off his clothes also, and prophesied before Samuel in like manner, and lay down naked all that day and all that night. Wherefore they say, Is Saul also among the prophets?

John 7

19 And Saul spake to Jonathan his son, and to all his servants, that they should kill David.

2 But Jonathan Saul's son delighted much in David: and Jonathan told David, saying, Saul my father seeketh to kill thee: now therefore, I pray thee, take heed to thyself until the morning, and abide in a secret place, and hide thyself:

3 And I will go out and stand beside my father in the field where thou art, and I will commune with my father of thee; and what I see, that I will tell thee.

4 And Jonathan spake good of David unto Saul his father, and said unto him, Let not the king sin against his servant, against David; because he hath not sinned against thee, and because his works have been to thee-ward very good:

5 For he did put his life in his hand, and slew the Philistine, and the LORD wrought a great salvation for all Israel: thou sawest it, and didst rejoice: wherefore then wilt thou sin against innocent blood, to slay David without a cause?

6 And Saul hearkened unto the voice of Jonathan: and Saul sware, As the LORD liveth, he shall not be slain.

7 And Jonathan called David, and Jonathan shewed him all those things. And Jonathan brought David to Saul, and he was in his presence, as in times past.

8 And there was war again: and David went out, and fought with the Philistines, and slew them with a great slaughter; and they fled from him.

9 And the evil spirit from the LORD was upon Saul, as he sat in his house with his javelin in his hand: and David played with his hand.

10 And Saul sought to smite David even to the wall with the javelin: but he slipped away out of Saul's presence, and he

smote the javelin into the wall: and David fled, and escaped that night.

11 Saul also sent messengers unto David's house, to watch him, and to slay him in the morning: and Michal David's wife told him, saying, If thou save not thy life to night, to morrow thou shalt be slain.

12 So Michal let David down through a window: and he went, and fled, and escaped.

13 And Michal took an image, and laid it in the bed, and put a pillow of goats' hair for his bolster, and covered it with a cloth.

14 And when Saul sent messengers to take David, she said, He is sick.

15 And Saul sent the messengers again to see David, saying, Bring him up to me in the bed, that I may slay him.

16 And when the messengers were come in, behold, there was an image in the bed, with a pillow of goats' hair for his bolster.

17 And Saul said unto Michal, Why hast thou deceived me so, and sent away mine enemy, that he is escaped? And Michal answered Saul, He said unto me, Let me go; why should I kill thee?

18 So David fled, and escaped, and came to Samuel to Ramah, and told him all that Saul had done to him. And he and Samuel went and dwelt in Naioth.

19 And it was told Saul, saying, Behold, David is at Naioth in Ramah.

²⁰ And Saul sent messengers to take David: and when they saw the company of the prophets prophesying, and Samuel standing as appointed over them, the Spirit of God was upon the messengers of Saul, and they also prophesied.

²¹ And when it was told Saul, he sent other messengers, and they prophesied likewise. And Saul sent messengers again the third time, and they prophesied also.

²² Then went he also to Ramah, and came to a great well that is in Sechu: and he asked and said, Where are Samuel and David? And one said, Behold, they be at Naioth in Ramah.

²³ And he went thither to Naioth in Ramah: and the Spirit of God was upon him also, and he went on, and prophesied, until he came to Naioth in Ramah.

²⁴ And he stripped off his clothes also, and prophesied before Samuel in like manner, and lay down naked all that day and all that night. Wherefore they say, Is Saul also among the prophets?

John 8

19 And Saul spake to Jonathan his son, and to all his servants, that they should kill David.

² But Jonathan Saul's son delighted much in David: and Jonathan told David, saying, Saul my father seeketh to kill thee: now therefore, I pray thee, take heed to thyself until the morning, and abide in a secret place, and hide thyself:

³ And I will go out and stand beside my father in the field where thou art, and I will commune with my father of thee; and what I see, that I will tell thee.

4 And Jonathan spake good of David unto Saul his father, and said unto him, Let not the king sin against his servant, against David; because he hath not sinned against thee, and because his works have been to thee-ward very good:

5 For he did put his life in his hand, and slew the Philistine, and the LORD wrought a great salvation for all Israel: thou sawest it, and didst rejoice: wherefore then wilt thou sin against innocent blood, to slay David without a cause?

6 And Saul hearkened unto the voice of Jonathan: and Saul sware, As the LORD liveth, he shall not be slain.

7 And Jonathan called David, and Jonathan shewed him all those things. And Jonathan brought David to Saul, and he was in his presence, as in times past.

8 And there was war again: and David went out, and fought with the Philistines, and slew them with a great slaughter; and they fled from him.

9 And the evil spirit from the LORD was upon Saul, as he sat in his house with his javelin in his hand: and David played with his hand.

10 And Saul sought to smite David even to the wall with the javelin: but he slipped away out of Saul's presence, and he smote the javelin into the wall: and David fled, and escaped that night.

11 Saul also sent messengers unto David's house, to watch him, and to slay him in the morning: and Michal David's wife told him, saying, If thou save not thy life to night, to morrow thou shalt be slain.

12 So Michal let David down through a window: and he went, and fled, and escaped.

¹³ And Michal took an image, and laid it in the bed, and put a pillow of goats' hair for his bolster, and covered it with a cloth.

¹⁴ And when Saul sent messengers to take David, she said, He is sick.

¹⁵ And Saul sent the messengers again to see David, saying, Bring him up to me in the bed, that I may slay him.

¹⁶ And when the messengers were come in, behold, there was an image in the bed, with a pillow of goats' hair for his bolster.

¹⁷ And Saul said unto Michal, Why hast thou deceived me so, and sent away mine enemy, that he is escaped? And Michal answered Saul, He said unto me, Let me go; why should I kill thee?

¹⁸ So David fled, and escaped, and came to Samuel to Ramah, and told him all that Saul had done to him. And he and Samuel went and dwelt in Naioth.

¹⁹ And it was told Saul, saying, Behold, David is at Naioth in Ramah.

²⁰ And Saul sent messengers to take David: and when they saw the company of the prophets prophesying, and Samuel standing as appointed over them, the Spirit of God was upon the messengers of Saul, and they also prophesied.

²¹ And when it was told Saul, he sent other messengers, and they prophesied likewise. And Saul sent messengers again the third time, and they prophesied also.

²² Then went he also to Ramah, and came to a great well that is in Sechu: and he asked and said, Where are Samuel and David? And one said, Behold, they be at Naioth in Ramah.

23 And he went thither to Naioth in Ramah: and the Spirit of God was upon him also, and he went on, and prophesied, until he came to Naioth in Ramah.

24 And he stripped off his clothes also, and prophesied before Samuel in like manner, and lay down naked all that day and all that night. Wherefore they say, Is Saul also among the prophets?

John 9

19 And Saul spake to Jonathan his son, and to all his servants, that they should kill David.

2 But Jonathan Saul's son delighted much in David: and Jonathan told David, saying, Saul my father seeketh to kill thee: now therefore, I pray thee, take heed to thyself until the morning, and abide in a secret place, and hide thyself:

3 And I will go out and stand beside my father in the field where thou art, and I will commune with my father of thee; and what I see, that I will tell thee.

4 And Jonathan spake good of David unto Saul his father, and said unto him, Let not the king sin against his servant, against David; because he hath not sinned against thee, and because his works have been to thee-ward very good:

5 For he did put his life in his hand, and slew the Philistine, and the LORD wrought a great salvation for all Israel: thou sawest it, and didst rejoice: wherefore then wilt thou sin against innocent blood, to slay David without a cause?

6 And Saul hearkened unto the voice of Jonathan: and Saul sware, As the LORD liveth, he shall not be slain.

⁷ And Jonathan called David, and Jonathan shewed him all those things. And Jonathan brought David to Saul, and he was in his presence, as in times past.

⁸ And there was war again: and David went out, and fought with the Philistines, and slew them with a great slaughter; and they fled from him.

⁹ And the evil spirit from the LORD was upon Saul, as he sat in his house with his javelin in his hand: and David played with his hand.

¹⁰ And Saul sought to smite David even to the wall with the javelin: but he slipped away out of Saul's presence, and he smote the javelin into the wall: and David fled, and escaped that night.

¹¹ Saul also sent messengers unto David's house, to watch him, and to slay him in the morning: and Michal David's wife told him, saying, If thou save not thy life to night, to morrow thou shalt be slain.

¹² So Michal let David down through a window: and he went, and fled, and escaped.

¹³ And Michal took an image, and laid it in the bed, and put a pillow of goats' hair for his bolster, and covered it with a cloth.

¹⁴ And when Saul sent messengers to take David, she said, He is sick.

¹⁵ And Saul sent the messengers again to see David, saying, Bring him up to me in the bed, that I may slay him.

¹⁶ And when the messengers were come in, behold, there was an image in the bed, with a pillow of goats' hair for his bolster.

¹⁷ And Saul said unto Michal, Why hast thou deceived me so, and sent away mine enemy, that he is escaped? And Michal answered Saul, He said unto me, Let me go; why should I kill thee?

¹⁸ So David fled, and escaped, and came to Samuel to Ramah, and told him all that Saul had done to him. And he and Samuel went and dwelt in Naioth.

¹⁹ And it was told Saul, saying, Behold, David is at Naioth in Ramah.

²⁰ And Saul sent messengers to take David: and when they saw the company of the prophets prophesying, and Samuel standing as appointed over them, the Spirit of God was upon the messengers of Saul, and they also prophesied.

²¹ And when it was told Saul, he sent other messengers, and they prophesied likewise. And Saul sent messengers again the third time, and they prophesied also.

²² Then went he also to Ramah, and came to a great well that is in Sechu: and he asked and said, Where are Samuel and David? And one said, Behold, they be at Naioth in Ramah.

²³ And he went thither to Naioth in Ramah: and the Spirit of God was upon him also, and he went on, and prophesied, until he came to Naioth in Ramah.

²⁴ And he stripped off his clothes also, and prophesied before Samuel in like manner, and lay down naked all that day and all that night. Wherefore they say, Is Saul also among the prophets?

III. CONCLUSION

Dear students, I pray you prosper and be in health as your soul propers (I pharaphrase.)[4] Study, study, study and I know that God will reward your efforts as you continue to

---

[4] "3 John 1:2 KJV: Beloved, I Wish above All Things That Thou Mayest Prosper and Be in Health, Even as Thy Soul Prospereth." *Bible Hub: Search, Read, Study the Bible in Many Languages*, https://biblehub.com/kjv/3_john/1-2.htm. Accessed 3 Mar. 2023.

study to show yourself approved a workman rightly dividing the Word of Truth that need not be ashamed.[5]

_____

[5] "2 Timothy 2:15 - Do Your Best to Present Yourself to God - Bible Gateway." *Bible Gateway,* https://www.biblegateway.com/passage/?search=2 Timothy 2:15. Accessed 3 Mar. 2023.

IIII. WORKS CITED

"Daniel 1 - Daniel's Training in Babylon - In the - Bible

    Gateway." *Bible Gateway*,

https://www.biblegateway.com/passage/?search=Daniel 1.

    Accessed 3 Mar. 2023.

"Daniel 2 - Nebuchadnezzar's Dream - In the - Bible Gateway." *Bible Gateway*, https://www.biblegateway.com/passage/?search=Daniel 2. Accessed 3 Mar. 2023.

"Daniel 2 - Nebuchadnezzar's Dream" *Bible Gateway*, https://www.biblegateway.com/passage/?search=Daniel 2. Accessed 3 Mar. 2023.

"Daniel 3 - The Image of Gold and the Blazing - Bible Gateway." *Bible Gateway*, https://www.biblegateway.com/passage/?search=Daniel 3. Accessed 3 Mar. 2023.

"DANIEL 3:25 KJV 'He Answered and Said, Lo, I See Four

Men Loose, Walking in the Midst of the Fire, and

They Have No Hurt;...'" *OFFICIAL KING JAMES*

BIBLE ONLINE: AUTHORIZED KING JAMES

VERSION

(KJV),
https://www.kingjamesbibleonline.org/Daniel-3-25/. Accessed

2 Mar. 2023.

IV. BIOGRAPHY OF Dr. Tasha Taylor

Has Doctorate from National School of Theology and accepted Jesus Christ as Lord and Savior.

Made in the USA
Columbia, SC
18 June 2024

b51c986b-5d8c-4571-94cc-197220337a93R01